Network Attacks & Exploitation

A Framework

Matthew Monte

WILEY

Network Attacks & Exploitation

Published by
John Wiley & Sons, Inc.
10475 Crosspoint Boulevard
Indianapolis, IN 46256
www.wiley.com

Copyright © 2015 by John Wiley & Sons, Inc., Indianapolis, Indiana

Published simultaneously in Canada

ISBN: 978-1-118-98712-4
ISBN: 978-1-118-98708-7 (ebk)
ISBN: 978-1-118-98723-0 (ebk)

10 9 8 7 6 5 4 3 2 1

For general information on our other products and services please contact our Customer Care Department within the United States at (877) 762-2974, outside the United States at (317) 572-3993 or fax (317) 572-4002.

Wiley publishes in a variety of print and electronic formats and by print-on-demand. Some material included with standard print versions of this book may not be included in e-books or in print-on-demand. If this book refers to media such as a CD or DVD that is not included in the version you purchased, you may download this material at http://booksupport.wiley.com. For more information about Wiley products, visit www.wiley.com.

Library of Congress Control Number: 2015941933

To those who toil in the shadows

About the Author

Matthew Monte is a security expert with 15 years' experience developing computer security tools and strategies for corporations and the U.S. government. His career includes technical and leadership positions in industry and the U.S. Intelligence Community. He holds a Master of Engineering in Computer Science from Cornell University.

About the Technical Editor

Dave Aitel started work for the NSA at age 18, long before anyone named Edward Snowden was a thing. Following that, he worked for @stake, and then started a company focused on offensive information security, Immunity, Inc.

Credits

Executive Editor
Carol Long

Project Editor
Tom Dinse

Technical Editor
Dave Aitel

Production Editor
Dassi Zeidel

Copy Editor
San Dee Phillips

**Manager of Content
Development & Assembly**
Mary Beth Wakefield

Marketing Director
David Mayhew

**Professional Technology &
Strategy Director**
Barry Pruett

Business Manager
Amy Knies

Associate Publisher
Jim Minatel

Project Coordinator, Cover
Brent Savage

Proofreader
Kathy Pope, Word One New York

Indexer
John Sleeva

Cover Designer
Michael E. Trent/Wiley

Cover Image
© iStock.com/Mak_Art

Acknowledgments

First and foremost, thank you to my beautiful wife Jessica. From the initial idea through the last review, this book would not have been possible without her encouragement and support. Thank you for being my sounding board and for taking on so much while I hid away behind my laptop.

Thank you to my children Annabelle and Levi, just for being you. You are the best kids a father could hope to have. Thank you for your smiles, patience, understanding, and welcome interruptions.

Thanks to my mother and departed father for their ever-present encouragement, including helping start my journey into the digital world long ago with a Commodore 64 and a guide to BASIC.

Thanks to everyone who contributed their time and effort including:

Dave Aitel, for agreeing to review this book and using his extensive experience to provide feedback and examples. This is a clearer, richer, and all-around better book for his challenging critiques and suggestions.

Carol Long, for seeing the potential in the early manuscript; to Tom Dinse for his guidance throughout the editing and publication process, and to the rest of the staff at Wiley for their diligent efforts.

David Nadwodny, for his thoughts and encouragement, and for demonstrating what can be accomplished with duct tape and string given ingenuity and initiative.

Dave N., for his thoughtful feedback early on that helped shape many of the presented ideas.

Finally, thank you to the people I did not name, those that I've worked with and learned so much from over the years, and those whose countless hours of research and analysis I relied upon. My gratitude to those that toil in the shadows, that try not, but do.

Contents

Introduction

Why are you arming, brother? And have you thought of sending someone to spy on the Trojans?

—Menelaus, the *Iliad*

Remember, hacking is more than just a crime. It's a survival trait.

—*Hackers* (1995)

This is not a book about Cyberwar, Cyber 9/11, or Cybergeddon. These terms are thrown about to generate page hits or to secure funding or business. They are designed to grab attention or shock you into action, and perhaps for that there is a use, but they are not particularly helpful in framing what to actually do about computer security. If Digital Pearl Harbor, a reference to a massive devastating surprise attack, is imminent, what must you do to prevent it? Update antivirus software? Be careful with attachments? Make sure your password has at least two n3mber5? The comparison to such events does not help you understand an attack or illuminate a strategy to prevent it.

Depending on what definition you use and who you ask, Cyberwar will never happen, is about to happen, or is already happening. Yet regardless of what verb tense is used for describing the state of Cyberwar, there is no question that cyber espionage is real and ongoing. Computer security companies meticulously detail immense spying campaigns with names such as Red October, Flame, or Aurora. Meanwhile the media runs story after story about the alleged capabilities of the National Security Agency and different Chinese PLA Units. While the meaning of Cyberwar is debated, the latest incarnation of an old profession is in full swing.

The sheer number of reported intrusions makes exploiting computer networks sound easy. The attackers are unattributable and unstoppable, the victims unwitting and powerless. In reading the news, you would think that every time a company loses its credit card data, discloses sensitive internal e-mails, or loses military secrets, the compromise was inevitable.

This attitude is lazy. The reasons given are invariably the same: an outdated system was neglected, a warning sign was missed, or a careless user exercised poor judgment. If only XYZ had been done, the attack would not have succeeded. And yet as countless companies and government agencies are repeatedly penetrated, it becomes clear that explaining what tactics were used is not good enough.

To understand the failure of computer security, you must move beyond analyzing a specific event to understanding the inherent properties of computer operations. Is there an intrinsic offensive advantage? What contributes or detracts from this advantage? What strategy must an attacker employ to remain successful? How can this strategy be countered? How can you keep pace with rapid technological change?

These are not easy questions. Answering them requires a framework for reasoning about the strategies, technologies, and methods for executing or defending against computer operations. This book attempts to form such a framework to address these and other questions, inferring and identifying those aspects of the subject that are enduring.

Computer espionage is increasing in frequency, sophistication, and impact. Political, military, intellectual property, personal, and financial information is being siphoned off at an unprecedented rate. As the legal and moral doctrines for dealing with this predicament emerge from infancy, the onslaught will continue. It is therefore critical for business leaders, IT professionals, and policy makers to start addressing the issues at a strategic level, and to do this, you first must understand the principles of network attack and exploitation.

Computer Network Exploitation

*A computer once beat me at chess, but it was
no match for me at kickboxing.*

—Emo Philips

Since Sun Tzu's *The Art of War,* historians and analysts have searched for guiding theories and principles of conflict. Their purpose was not always to create some academic treatise to be beheld or to provide an endless stream of pithy quotes for marketing presentations. Rather, in exploring the principles of conflict, the goal is to confer an advantage in training, planning, research and development, execution, and defense—in short, to increase the efficiency and effectiveness of a fighting force in all aspects.

Information systems are a new area of conflict; one in which the incursions are virtual and the violations of sovereignty are abstracted. Yet the stakes are tangible. There may be no land involved, but both sides seek to attack and protect a territory and property.

Information systems are integrated into all aspects of the global economy and modern nation-states. Of course, there is e-mail and the Web, but less visible are the inventory, ordering, and payment systems that drive business. You barely notice when the grocery store prints out coupons based on your shopping habits, while simultaneously noting the inventory loss for later restocking. All this data is shared over a network and stored in a data center in…well…you actually have no idea. Yet this unseen database can reveal not only your favorite item from aisle 10, but also whether you are married, have kids, own pets, like to drink, or are out of town right now.

Now the flavor of ice cream you prefer may not be much of a secret worth stealing, but there is a wealth of information that is. Interested in how to log in to a bank by spoofing someone's supposedly secure login token? Looking to know which of your neighbors are dissidents and are "inciting subversion of the state"? Curious about what an aspiring U.S. vice presidential candidate writes in e-mails? Do you find the source code to the computer systems on the F-35 Joint Strike Fighter appealing? My mint chocolate chip preference is the only untouched thing on this list; though that too is questionable.

Given the huge potential economic and military benefits of acquiring this information, it's no surprise that the act of stealing computer information has become a well-funded profession. And like any profession, it has developed its own set of terminology. So before getting too deep, let's start with the basics.

Computer Network Exploitation (CNE) is computer espionage, the stealing of information. It encompasses gaining access to computer systems and retrieving data. An old analogy is that of a cold war spy who picks the lock on a house, sneaks in, takes pictures of documents with his secret camera, and gets out without leaving a trace. A more modern analogy would be a drone that invades a hostile country's airspace to gather intelligence on troop strength.

Computer Network Attack (CNA) is akin to a traditional military attack or sabotage. It applies the four D's of "disrupt, deny, degrade, or destroy" to computer networks. Now, the cold war spy smashes a few artifacts as he leaves or maybe *Fight Club*-style, he introduces a gas leak so that the whole place explodes sometime later. Meanwhile, the drone rains hellfire missiles. CNA is the computer equivalent. It describes actions and effects that range from the subtle to the catastrophic.

Non-kinetic Computer Network Attack is a term this book uses to describe the subset of CNA conducted virtually, that is, any disruption, denial, degradation, or destruction initiated and performed via computers or computer networks. Although sending a missile into a data center is a rather effective form of CNA that fits well within the definition, physically initiated acts are outside the scope of this book.

Non-kinetic CNA therefore describes damage with virtual causes; though there very well may be physical effects. To continue with the analogy, instead of breaking anything, the spy remotely shuts off the heat during an extremely cold night causing the water pipes to burst. The cause was virtual, but the effect was not.

Computer Network Defense (CND) is protecting your networks from being exploited or attacked. It's the locks, doors, walls, and windows on the house and the police officer that walks by once a day on her beat, or the radar sweeps and antiaircraft missile systems that line the border.

Like CNA, there are both physical and virtual aspects to CND, but the term generally applies only to virtual security and is therefore used that way in this book.

Finally, *Computer Network Operations* (*CNO*) is the umbrella term that is composed of all the previous terms: Computer Network Exploitation (CNE), Computer Network Attack (CNA), and Computer Network Defense (CND).

CNE is the key subject necessary for understanding all aspects of the topic. As shown in Figure 1.1, the effective parts of each discipline are rooted in CNE.

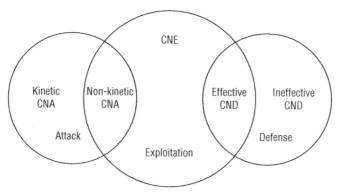

Figure 1.1: CNO disciplines

Effective non-kinetic CNA requires at least a measure of access to the target. Generally, the more access you have, the wider the range of options available. With minimal access, you might temporarily take a website offline. With extensive access, you can erase the data on tens of thousands of computers and take the company down for a week, as was done to the oil company Saudi Aramco, allegedly by Iran.

CND, or defense, does not rely directly on CNE (at least not while it remains illegal to counterattack), but trying to craft a successful network defense without understanding the offense is like trying to design a flak jacket without any knowledge of ballistics. Either way, the exercise is going to end with something full of holes.

CNE is central and therefore worth formally defining. The U.S. Department of Defense defines CNE as

> *Enabling operations and intelligence collection capabilities conducted through the use of computer networks to gather data from target or adversary automated information systems or networks.*

> —*Joint Publication 3-13*

The first thing to note is that CNE is directed. There is a "target or adversary." This is a differentiating factor. Many a computer worm or virus, such as Michelangelo, Code Red, Melissa, or SQL Slammer, has gained access to computer systems. And yet, these infections were not CNE because there was no intended target and no intent to gather information.

An indiscriminate worm is more like the flu. There is no conscious choice of victim, and whether a particular person gets sick is a combination of natural defenses, preparation, and luck. CNE is more like biological warfare, leveraged with a particular target in mind.

This is not to say that a CNE operation is always precision targeted or that it will never compromise a collateral computer. Counterexamples exist. Stuxnet was a wormlike attack that infiltrated Iranian nuclear facilities and then went on to infect other companies. Worms, like those created to exploit the Linux Shellshock vulnerability, can be leveraged to deposit backdoors in preparation for later access. Every action need not be deterministic, but on balance, the bulk of a CNE operation is intended to be focused, targeted, and invisible.

The rest of the Department of Defense's definition provides a good basis for discussion but requires one significant point of emphasis. To understand the missing nuance, you must first understand computer operations.

Operations

A *CNE operation* is a series of coordinated actions directed toward a target computer or network in furtherance of a mission objective. The mission objective may be anything ranging from political intelligence, design plans, company strategies, or plain-old financial information.

Let's parse this definition because several words take on different meanings in a CNE context.

The word *target* has an intentional duality. Whether target systems, target networks, target data, or target employees, "target" simultaneously refers to both the goal and the obstacles to reaching it. Target includes both the data you want to acquire and the forces in place to protect it.

Though the word *attacker* is commonly used to describe the offensive actor, the corresponding *defender* is notably absent from this definition. A target might defend, but it might not. A target may not even know if and when it is attacked.

Now everyone knows what a computer is, right? It's a desktop, laptop, or smartphone. True. But it's also your television, alarm system, building air conditioning system, and increasingly your car. So you must consider a computer in general terms. A *computer* is any device that contains or can be leveraged to access wanted data.

A computer can be a target, an attacker, or both at the same time. The same computer can run a defensive security product and a program designed to circumvent that very product. Computers are not on one side of the attacker/

target relationship any more than a chessboard is on the side of the black or white pieces. Certain squares start out under the control of one side or the other, but as the game progresses, it is not going to stay that way.

A *computer network* is a hierarchy of connected computers controlled by one entity. Computer networks can be simple or complex, ranging from two computers connected by a single cable to millions connected across satellite links and oceans.

Networks are made up of both computers and network devices. A *network device* is any device whose purpose is to facilitate or inhibit communication. Simple network devices are like a house circuit breaker. Electricity, or in this case data, comes in, is potentially transformed, and routed out the appropriate path. Examples include cable modems, DSL converters, and Wi-Fi access points.

More sophisticated network devices not only route data, but also can selectively grant, monitor, or deny access based on the type of data and its destination. Examples include smart switches, routers, and firewalls. These network devices are sophisticated enough that they can be considered just a specialized class of computers.

One final definition needed, though not explicitly included in operations, is the Internet. The *Internet* is a large system of networks linked together, but with no common entity controlling access. It is a series of contradictions: simultaneously concentrated and dispersed, interconnected and segmented, and established but under constant change. It is conceptually simple yet enormously complex in architecture, design, and regulation.

Within a CNE operation, an attacker is not concerned about the entirety of the Internet, but only the attacker's own network, the target network, and any intermediary devices, networks, or services connecting the two. Thus, you can view the Internet as a means of communication for carrying out a mission's objective.

Operational Objectives

All CNE operations have an operational objective, or put simply, a goal. The specific objectives vary widely with the actors and their capabilities, but the types of objectives are common. Operational objectives can be broadly divided into the five categories shown in Figure 1.2.

An operation falls into one or more of these categories at any given point in time. Operations, though, are not static. An operation may begin as firmly fixed in one category, but change over time or with a change of circumstances. The arrows in Figure 1.2 denote how this form of mission creep typically proceeds.

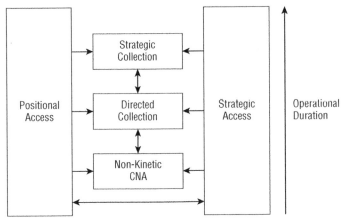

Figure 1.2: Operational categories

Strategic Collection

Strategic collection operations target the collection of economic, political, financial, military, or other information for strategic reasons. The aim of strategic collection is not one particular piece of data, but rather the collection of data *over time* that you can analyze to determine power shifts, plans, trends, adversarial capabilities, and so on.

For example, according to WikiLeaks, the NSA has been recording nearly all phone conversations in Afghanistan.[1] This is a perfect illustration of strategic collection. This collection may reveal the strength and plans of various warlords, the low-level leadership structure of any remaining Al-Qaeda, or perhaps any shifts in government corruption. Each of these is a strategic intelligence requirement for the U.S. government.

Strategic collection may also lead to tactical information. In this example, monitoring the communications of a particular warlord to understand regional stability is a strategic objective, but doing so may provide actionable tactical information that can be used to intercept a weapons shipment coming in from Pakistan. This information could tip off analysts to other targets of interest, giving birth to a directed collection operation.

Strategic collection requires substantial analytic capabilities for success because there may be an enormous amount of information to sort through, and the exact nature of what is useful may be unknown. There are somewhere in the neighborhood of 20 million mobile phone subscribers in Afghanistan.[2] If we assume each subscriber makes only a single 1-minute phone call each day to another subscriber, then recording every call requires processing and storing 10 million minutes of audio, or about 19 years' worth, every day. This much data is worthless unless analysis can be automated.

Due to the cost and sheer technical magnitude of strategic collection, this objective is limited to nation-states or well-funded criminal organizations.

Directed Collection

Directed collection operations target the collection of information to meet an immediate objective. The nature of the wanted information, or at a minimum the general class of it, is known from the beginning.

For example, China is alleged to have stolen the plans to the next-generation Patriot Missile system, a so-called aerial interceptor, or system that knocks incoming missiles out of the sky. Imagine that someone shoots a bullet at you. Now imagine trying to hit that bullet with another bullet, and you can get some sense of the amount of advanced engineering and technology that must go into these types of systems. This is a worthy target of interest.

Of course, there is no way to know whether the Chinese specifically sought out these plans or just happened upon them, but it seems more likely than not that it was a directed effort. China's military would be keenly interested in both building its own versions and studying ways to defeat them.

This is the essence of directed collection. The target was known: the U.S. Defense contractor Raytheon or any of its suppliers and partners. And the general class of information was known: weapons system data. It was likely just the specifics of which network to go after, the type of data to search for, and so forth that were learned after the operation commenced.

A weapons system is just one example. Financial and credit card data is a common goal of criminal directed collection. Customer lists and e-mail addresses are another. A specific person's skype communications may be yet another. The common thread is a priori knowledge of the end goal.

But as noted previously, strategic collection can result in this type of information. So what's the difference between strategic and directed collection? The only differences between the two are the initial intent of the operation and the duration.

Because directed collection operations seek specific information, the operation may end after that information is obtained. Does this sound likely though? Does anyone believe that the Chinese are going to walk away from whatever systems they compromised containing weapons design plans? Of course not.

In practice, directed collecting is extended. If useful information is gathered once from a target, that target is likely to contain useful information again. For another example, why would a criminal steal one batch of credit cards, say from eBay, and then stop if he could remain undetected and harvest more credit cards later? Answer: he wouldn't.

Directed collection operations may begin with a short life expectancy, but successful operations will be extended over time.

Non-Kinetic Computer Network Attack (CNA)

Non-kinetic CNA operations are meant to disrupt, deny, degrade, or destroy the operational capability of a computer network. The extreme examples are often portrayed in the media: the vulnerability of the power grid, the air traffic control system, river dam controls, and such. The fear is that some nefarious actor can cause devastating physical consequences. There is an element of truth in this, enough to make it a real security issue, but the reality of non-kinetic CNA operations to date has been much less spectacular. More often than not a website is just knocked offline for a day or two.

The methods of non-kinetic CNA can be divided into two general categories: attacks conducted from outside the target network without access and those conducted from inside with access.

Attacking from the outside of a network without access is relatively common. Amazon.com, Yahoo, eBay, Microsoft, and pretty much every major company with an e-commerce website have had their networks degraded by attackers leveraging thousands of computers in Distributed Denial of Service (DDOS) attacks.

DDOS attacks have been used against nations as well. In 2007, an attack disrupted much of Estonia's government, finance, and news outlets. And in 2008, another attack took down services in Georgia, ever so coincidentally timed a few weeks before Russia invaded part of it. The attacks may have been perpetrated by Russia or by cyber-rioters as the Russians claimed—an interesting question itself—but the fact that a nation-state's electronic governmental and commercial infrastructure was attacked and degraded is not in dispute.

DDOS attacks require a substantial number of computers to launch. If attackers owned or leased thousands of computers, they could do it themselves, but realistically, DDOS attacks are launched from *botnets*, a network of often thousands of third-party computers where attackers have *durable* access and control.

Outside attacks, though often effective, suffer from several disadvantages. They are easily detected. The disruption lasts only as long as the attack is active. They have no impact on the sensitive core of a network. There is little if any lasting damage, and recovery is almost immediate as soon as the attack subsides. Finally, the attack may steam roll innocent third parties that just happen to be in the way.

Non-kinetic CNA launched from inside the network provides a much wider range of options. Attacks can be subtle and difficult to detect. They have the potential to reach more sensitive or critical systems or data. Damage can be severe and last well beyond the duration of the attack. Recovery can be expensive and time-consuming. Finally, an inside attack can be tailored and highly targeted to reduce collateral damage and the impact to untargeted systems.

The fist reported large-scale example of this kind of attack had all these qualities. In 2010, the world was introduced to Stuxnet, a tailored attack against Iran. The attack software spread via 0-days, unknown and unpatched vulnerabilities, to reach its ultimate target: the programmable logic controllers that control Iranian centrifuges. When installed, the program subtly modified the controllers in a way that caused the centrifuges to break. This first-of-its-kind attack reportedly damaged 20 percent of Iranian centrifuges before it was detected. At that point, it had been in progress for at least 1 year, with components of the software under development for at least 5 years.

A couple of years later the Wiper malware struck in two separate incidents. The first incident was against the oil company Saudi Aramco in 2012. The second was against various South Korean financial and media companies in 2013. The Wiper program spread by stealing and using credentials, and then, depending on the variant, either immediately or at the appointed time wiping critical sections of the infected computers to make them unbootable. Subtle it was not.

This type of non-kinetic CNA done with access exhibited by Stuxnet and Wiper is far more effective than an outside attack, but also far more difficult and expensive. It first requires gaining access to the target network. This makes the first part of the operation effectively identical to strategic or directed collection. Access must be gained for all of them. The only difference is that the access is leveraged to cause damage rather than gather information.

Strategic Access

Strategic access operations are executed for the purpose of future flexibility. Unlike strategic collection, it is unknown but hoped that the access will become useful at some point later. The access may lead to strategic or directed collection, non-kinetic CNA opportunities—or nothing at all. The attacker simply does not know at the onset.

In 2013, it was reported that GCHQ, Britain's signals intelligence service, hacked Belgium telecom provider Belgacom. This seems like a logical strategic access operation. Gaining access to this company might enable collection against European governmental organizations or diplomats within Brussels. Or it might open up opportunities to eavesdrop on or manipulate communications that traverse Belgacom's International Carrier Services, which, as the name implies, provides wholesale carrier services to countries around the world. This is, of course, complete speculation, but it fits the pattern of a useful strategic access operation.

Other examples of this operational objective are harder to come by, as their nature is to lie in wait and take minimal action. Still, it is plain to see that a strategic access operation is most useful if the access is *extended* if and until that access proves useful.

Positional Access

Positional access operations target computers and networks that are not themselves of interest but are useful in furthering a different objective.

An example of positional access is gaining access to the home computer of an employee of a target company. The computer itself may be of no interest, but perhaps the employee connects into the target company from home. This is exactly how Microsoft was hacked some 15 years ago. Positional access via the employee's computer provided an avenue for an attacker to circumvent Microsoft's perimeter security.

This method was also used to compromise the department store Target in late 2013. As shown in Figure 1.3, the intruders first compromised one of Target's suppliers, an HVAC vendor. They then used that vendor's credentials to compromise Target itself and make off with some 40 million credit card numbers.

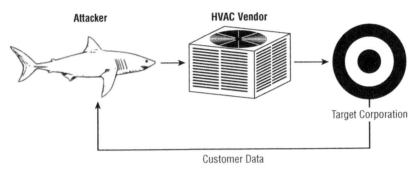

Figure 1.3: Positional access

Another example of positional access is compromising a university network to launch an attack. Again, the university network itself is of no interest, but it provides a layer of anonymity to an attacker. Some organizations, notably GCHQ according to the Snowden documents, allegedly proactively scan for vulnerable hosts they can add to their real estate portfolio for later use.

By attacking through these intermediaries, it will be more difficult for the target to trace the origin of the attack. This explains why China allegedly hacked a mental health clinic in California. It makes a suitable intra-U.S. launching point. It also explains why the Chinese offensive organization PLA 61398, a.k.a. APT1, purchased or leased hundreds of servers spread throughout 13 countries. Why bother compromising an intermediary when you can just buy one?

Positional access operations, like directed collection, may begin with a specific intent and a short life expectancy. However, just like directed collection, these operations may be extended. The employee's home computer may be needed if an attacker ever loses access to the target organization's network. Access to the mental clinic or a leased server could be used to launch several operations.

That said, out of all the operational objectives, extending positional access carries the most risk. The access may prove useful, but it may link together different operations if one is discovered. This is a calculated risk each attacker must weigh.

CNE Revisited

In each of the five operational objectives—strategic collection, directed collection, non-kinetic CNA, strategic access, and positional access—the likely success of the operation is linked to its duration. Extended access yields greater potential for gathering useful data in strategic collection, a potentially constant stream of updating information for directed collection, and a larger window of opportunity and a wider range of options for performing non-kinetic CNA. Extended access increases the likelihood that the systems compromised for strategic access or for positional access become or remain useful.

In short, almost all operations, independent of objective, are more likely to enjoy greater degrees of success if access can be sustained. Therefore, when thinking about strategy, a more useful definition of CNE than the one presented earlier in the chapter is

> *Sustained* *enabling operations and intelligence collection capabilities conducted through the use of computer networks to gather data from target or adversary automated information systems or networks.*

This small addition of one word makes a large difference in fashioning a framework. Sustaining an operation is not easy. It adds an order of magnitude of complexity over simply gaining access. Yet sustained access is the key to both strategic and tactical success. It is the true art of CNE.

Construing CNE to emphasize duration also has the welcome side effect of marginalizing the attention-seeking behavior such as that shown by various "hacker" groups or self-appointed electronic armies. There's no real strategy behind defacing a few websites. Media coverage is anathema to sustained access and thus to CNE.

Though as duration is stressed, some operations will be intentionally short-lived. Perhaps there is only one useful piece of data to gain from a network. Maybe circumstances change and the political risk of exposure suddenly outweighs the benefits of the information. There are always exceptions. However, frameworks must be developed around the expected case. With such structure in hand, it becomes clearer why the special cases are indeed special.

And for CNE, as with anything that yields political, military, or economic advantages, the expected case is that operations are rarely willfully abandoned.

A Framework for Computer Network Exploitation

The tactics of CNE ebb and flow, but certain aspects of the discipline remain constant. These tenets can structure your thinking and help provide direction to both offensive and defensive actors. The tenets of CNE can be divided into three categories based on their respective expected durability: first principles, principles, and themes.

First Principles

First principles are immutable and fundamental. They transcend the constantly shifting technology they seek to describe. For CNE, there are three such foundational supports, which are the principles of access, humanity, and economy.

- **Humanity**—CNE is grounded in human nature.[3] Although it is a highly technical domain, the technology is designed, built, used, and monitored by humans. The most sophisticated technology in the world is envisioned, brought to life, and in CNE, torn apart by people. As Carl von Clausewitz (Prussian general) noted for war, "[Theory] must also take the human factor into account, and find room for courage, boldness, and even foolhardiness."

- **Access**—There is always someone with legitimate access and a means to use it.[4] Whether it's the president of the United States and nuclear launch codes, the bank manager and the vault, or me and my collection of decorative soaps, there is someone with access to everything that is secured. Data is no different. It does not exist in a vacuum. It is generated and stored for the express purpose of being accessed later by someone with legitimate access.

- **Economy**—Ambitions always exceed available resources.[3] Whether it's a nation's foreign policy goals, an educational board's budget outline, the charity one supports, or just the kind of car one wants to buy, there are more goals than people, expertise, time, money, or technology can support. The same is true for both computer offense and defense. There is a priority, cost, and benefit to every action and to every outcome.

Principles

Principles shed light on various aspects of a subject. They are not universal truths, but as Clausewitz stated, "intended to provide a thinking man with a frame of reference." They are tools to "stimulate and serve as a guide for reflection."[5]

Principles may change, albeit slowly, as circumstances or perspectives change. For example, the U.S. Army used to expound the war principle of *cooperation*, but in 1949, it replaced it with *unity of command*. This change of principles and doctrine reflected changing circumstances, mainly the advances in communication that allowed real-time information to flow between physically separated units and commanders. Cooperation bacame less important if a well-informed hierarchy was in place to see the big picture.

Principles may also be redefined. The war principle of *mass* was derived from ancient times, and the idea of massing forces, that is, people, at the critical point of a battle. If the general could bring more soldiers than his enemy to bear in the right place and time, he was likely to prevail. However, with the increasing power and range of weapons over the centuries, concentrating forces at a single point was a recipe for annihilation. Rather than abandoning it outright, the Army reinterpreted the principle to mean the massing of combat power instead, that is, the focusing of ground, sea, and air capabilities at the decisive point.

Still, principles are more than just passing fads. A good principle will withstand evolutionary changes in technology. There are currently six principles of CNE, shown supported by the three first principles (access, humanity, economy) in Figure 1.4.

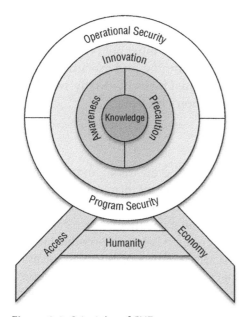

Figure 1.4: Principles of CNE

In brief, the principles are

- **Knowledge**—The broad and deep understanding of computers and computer networks, as well as the behavioral and psychological characteristics of people and organizations.

- **Awareness**—The mapping of the operational domain, including the active detection and monitoring of events in near real time.

- **Innovation**—The ability to create new technology, leverage existing technologies, or develop and adapt operational methods to new circumstances.

- **Precaution**—The minimization of the impact of unwitting actions on an operation.

- **Operational Security**—The minimization of defender exposure, recognition, and reaction to the existence of an operation.

- **Program Security**—The containment of damage caused by the compromise of an operation.

Together these principles form an ideal offensive goal, a target as it were. They are all interrelated. Some offer synergy. The first principles support everything, with humanity as the crucial connector. Knowledge is central to all of the other rings. Increased innovation improves every principle it touches.

Other principles trade off against each other. Operational security and program security are often at odds. The greater awareness one has, the less need for precaution and vice versa.

The principles will be explored in depth in Chapter 7, "Offensive Strategy," but for now, it is enough to understand that sometimes principles are in concert and other times they are in conflict. That is why principles must not be considered goals in and of themselves. They are a guide to planning and execution. Each operation is unique, and the equities involved must be individually weighed and continually balanced throughout the operation's lifetime.

Themes

Themes are reoccurring ideas that often underlie the means of an operation. They are like the theme song to a movie, found in different forms over and over again throughout the picture. Themes are useful to help quickly determine a suitable course of action in consideration of a strategic principle.

In an ideal world, you could catalog and reference a list of all possible tactics and quickly choose among them as the need arises. This works for a static and finite problem, such as tic-tac-toe or Connect Four, but the number of tactics and the speed and variability of technological change make such an approach impossible. You must therefore resort to using themes, a form of distilled operational experience.

Themes have more staying power than a specific tactic. Common themes include:

- **Diversity**—Leveraging a wide range of tools, technologies, development methods, network signatures, infrastructure, and operational methods

- **Stealth**—Leveraging tools, technologies, and methods that are largely hidden from view, or if in view, unlikely to attract attention

- **Redundancy**—Reasonable fail-safes, backups, and contingency plans for foreseeable setbacks and obstacles

Themes make poor stand-alone goals without principles and context. Stealth, for example, has no meaning unless one defines from what and for what purpose.

To make everything redundant without the context of what is at risk is to make everything prohibitively expensive.

Themes must always be considered within the broader strategic context. For example, developing a CNE capability against Blackberry devices may improve an attacker's technical diversity. The collection method may be stealthy. And it may offer redundancy into accessing someone's e-mail. But developing such a capability is a poor strategic move because as Blackberry's market share continues to plummet compared to iPhone and Android devices, the number of interesting targets using Blackberry devices will diminish. (That said, if a high-priority target shows no sign of abandoning them, then perhaps it is worth the investment.)

There are other themes as well that one may discover better suit a given organization, such as speed of execution or automation of tasks. Regardless, a diverse, stealthy, and redundant collection of tactics provides an incredibly powerful weapon for any attacker. With the right strategy, few defenses can withstand it.

Summary

Computer Network Exploitation is but the latest reincarnation of espionage. As an increasing part of the world's political, economic, and military information is stored on networks, a framework for organizing and analyzing CNE becomes necessary to national security.

Though CNE motivations and objectives are essentially infinite, operations can be grouped into one of five general categories: strategic collection, directed collection, non-kinetic CNA, strategic access, and positional access. Regardless of category, sustaining an operation likely leads to greater success.

CNE may be a fast-moving technological field, but some aspects are enduring. These are worth identifying, as they can help you derive strategies for building, planning, and executing operations or for defending against those that are.

The next chapter explores how the offense is guided by these principles.

The Attacker

You're gonna need a bigger boat.

—Jaws

The offense is routinely underestimated. When companies are hacked, they react as if they had only done this one thing or avoided this one mistake everything would have been okay. The adversary is treated as if they just got lucky. So another hole is patched, another finger put into the dike, and the exploited company continues onward, utterly surprised the next time it is hacked.

The offense is routinely overestimated. When companies are hacked, they react as if it was inevitable, that no amount of effort could have prevented it. They resign themselves to cleaning up the mess and waiting for the next time, secure in the hopeless certainty there will be a next time.

The truth is that the offense is neither lucky nor invincible, but they are successful. To break their winning streak, you must step back and understand the attacker and the nature of operations. The same is true for the opposite motivation: If people want to extend the winning streak and attack more effectively, they must understand how they are guided and restricted by the first principles of Computer Network Exploitation (CNE).

Principle of Humanity

CNE is grounded in human nature.

The attacker is a person or a group of people. The attacker may be a lone actor, a well-ordered hierarchy, or a loose conglomeration of thousands, but regardless the attacker is human. For this reason, from now on this book uses the proper noun "Attacker" as a reminder that there are people behind it all.

Attacker motivations are many and varied. Internet vandals may attack systems just for kicks or to make a political statement. Criminals look to make money. Nations gather intelligence to seek military advantage, to track down terrorist plots, or to counter drug smuggling, among other things. These are all human motivations. Indeed the true objective of any CNE operation is ultimately human in nature.

For the Attacker, thinking of operations in terms of the human objectives frees them from becoming narrowly focused on trying to create perfect technical solutions. Good enough should suffice as long as the objective is met.

For the Defender, understanding that the Attacker is human opens a wider range of options. No longer are we battling Trojans and other faceless programs. There is a real adversary to be reckoned with, and the countermeasures can be technical, political, legal, or economic. Just imagine if the next time Amazon were hacked it decided to raise prices across the board at the Chinese site Amazon.cn. Would this have an effect? Maybe. Maybe not. But until one starts thinking of the Attacker as a group of people, these types of creative solutions will never enter people's consciousness.

Although Attackers and their motivations are quite human, the means of an operation seem the opposite, completely technical. Attacker tools that elevate privileges, capture keystrokes, or look for payment information in memory, to name but a few, are all technical—so are the things these tools exploit: web browsers, databases, network protocols, operating systems, and more. Defensive tools such as firewalls, intrusion prevention systems, antivirus software, and enterprise management systems are also just as technical.

Yet all these technical tools, from the most basic to the most complex, reflect the expertise and biases of the humans that developed them. From the industrial control system created with no concept of being networked to the supercool smartphone app pushed out to market without a second thought about security, the marks of the designers are left throughout. And because of this reflection, like their creators, the technology is full of flaws.

The Attacker that can understand the paradox of the humanity infused into technology will think like its creators, will see their assumptions, and will find ways to violate those assumptions to great effect. Likewise, the Defender that sees the humanity of the Attacker can begin to counter the actual problem instead of going after the Hydra's latest head.

Life Cycle of an Operation

Before diving into the other first principles of CNE, you must first understand the typical sustained operational life cycle. The stages of an offensive operation are targeting, initial access, persistence, expansion, exfiltration, and detection, as shown in Figure 2.1.

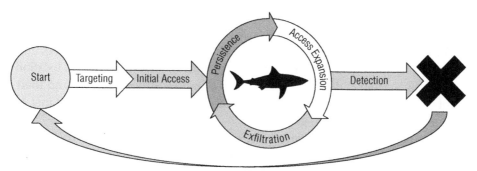

Figure 2.1: Ideal operational life cycle

Although it is often useful to think of the stages as discreet steps, one leading to another, this is inaccurate. Each stage often remains ongoing throughout the entire operation. The true life cycle of an operation is more like Figure 2.2—a tangled mess.

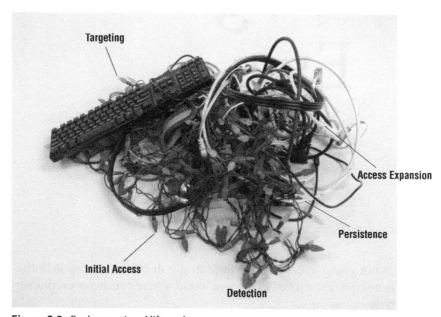

Figure 2.2: Real operational life cycle

Stage 1: Targeting

Targeting can be broken into two distinct parts: identification of the target network and identifying the attack strategies and tactics necessary to exploit that network. It is the difference between figuring out which bank to rob and then determining how to rob it.

Identifying a target network is not necessarily easy. For example, suppose you were interested in the design of an adversary's new weapons system. Where would you start? To identify the key computer networks, you might need to understand the organizational structure of the armed forces, determine the physical location of where the system is designed, or identify potential subcontractors and their organizational structures. All this information is potentially required just to figure out which network to go after.

Unfortunately, there's not much the targeted can do to disrupt this stage. Much of the initial targeting can take place without ever touching the network, and there are no available tools that can notify an organization that someone is gathering information about it elsewhere, except maybe AdWords. I can just imagine the marketing campaign in Figure 2.3.

Figure 2.3: Unlikely products

Clearly this is not going to happen. So targeting will remain invisible to the targeted. This is notably in contrast to the real world where countersurveillance is an important defensive measure.

During targeting, some targets are sought out, but the target identification process may also work in reverse. Targeting can be opportunistic. The Attacker identifies a weakness or a working attack strategy and then searches for vulnerable networks. The access is established first and the objective afterward. This is especially useful for strategic access operations where the specific objective may not be known.

Imagine a criminal that knows how to unlock and hot-wire a Trans Am. She won't wait for a particular person to buy one. Instead, she would go to a mall parking lot and seek out victims. Depending on a host of factors, the thief may just open the cars and search for money, or perhaps if conditions permit, she would steal one and sell it. The exact goal of the operation is unknown at the onset, but there is a known vulnerability, a capability, and hope.

Sometime in 2009, a few Romanians compromised the sandwich chain Subway. Over the next 2 years, they managed to steal somewhere between $3 million and $10 million, an amount that would allow them to eat fresh for quite some time. How did they do it? As reported by *Wired*[1]:

> *The hackers allegedly scanned the internet to identify vulnerable POS systems with certain remote desktop software applications installed on them, and then used the applications to log into the targeted POS system, either by guessing the passwords or using password-cracking software.*

Our presumably hungry foes used opportunistic targeting. They had a known vulnerability and sought out a vulnerable system. It could have just as easily been Jimmy John's, PF Chang's, or Dairy Queen, all of which were also compromised in the last 2 years.

Of course, the victims may not care whether they were specifically targeted or were just a target of opportunity. The losses are the same. But they should care. If someone has his car stolen, it makes a big difference whether it was intentionally sought out or just left in the wrong place. The answer speaks to the likelihood of having the next car stolen. It also indicates whether he should focus more on the car's inherent security features or on where he parks.

Some companies do not believe they will be targeted because they are uninteresting or have little of value. There is something intuitive to this line of thinking. I used exactly this thought process for deciding never to bother locking the doors of my first car, a machine that was literally held together by coat hangers, duct tape, and staples. I reasoned that if someone were going to steal a car, they would steal a better car than mine.

But while decidedly true for my lemon, the "better car" theory of security breaks down when attacks can be automated and there is a potential positional use for every point of access. Yes, Olivia, you are a target whether or not you think you have anything worthwhile.

Targeting does not end after a network is identified. The Attacker must determine the plan and layout the tactics necessary to successfully execute and sustain the operation. This may be easy if the network were opportunistically found, but it's not as straightforward otherwise.

Targeting at this stage includes gathering technical information, like the public network presence or the software the organization uses. This is used to attack the organization from the outside in.

Targeting also includes nontechnical information such as the names, e-mail addresses, and tastes of employees. Phishing e-mails, the targeted e-mail attacks that entice a user to go to a website or perform some other action, require knowing where to cast and what to use as bait.

For example, according to *Slate* magazine[2], the Associated Press had its Twitter account compromised with this short e-mail:

From: [An AP staffer]

Subject: News

Hello,

Please read the following article, it's very important:

http://www.washingtonpost.com/blogs/worldviews/wp/2013/04/23

This simple and direct lure required knowing the name and e-mail address of the sending AP staffer, as well as the e-mail address(es) of the recipients, information almost certainly gathered without ever touching an Associated Press computer.

Targeting yields a series of contingencies for gaining initial access to the network. But even when one of these plans is successful, and a network is breached, targeting does not stop. In 2010, when the NASDAQ stock market exchange was compromised:

The agents figured the hackers first broke into Nasdaq's computers at least three months before they were detected, but that was just a guess.

—Businessweek[3]

Goodwill Industries was compromised for at least a full year and a half before anyone noticed. During this time, the Attacker most certainly continued targeting and retargeting, watching for how the network was changing, looking for another way in or out, or for another place to hide, just in case.

Targeting may be the first stage but it is also continual.

Stage 2: Initial Access

Initial access consists of penetrating any defensive security and gaining the ability to run commands or other software on one of the target's computers or network devices. This can be accomplished through exploiting vulnerabilities, leveraging network misconfigurations, social engineering, or many other means, some of which are discussed in the "Access" section later in this chapter.

Gaining initial access is the most glorified and media-hyped stage of an operation, but it is also the shortest and often the easiest.

As shown in Figure 2.4, according to the National Institute of Science and Technology (NIST) National Vulnerability Database[4], the number of new reported vulnerabilities has remained around 5,000 per year for the past 5 years.

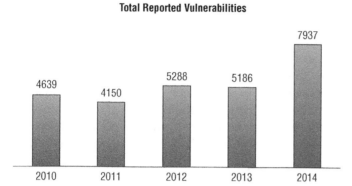

Figure 2.4: Total vulnerabilities

The vulnerabilities are scored based on a number of factors including whether they require local or remote access, the ease of exploitation, whether the Attacker must be authenticated, the impact to the integrity of the system, and so forth. The most dangerous vulnerabilities, the type often used to gain initial access, are rated "high severity," defined as 7 or above on a 10-point scale. These vulnerabilities are showing no signs of slowing down either as shown in Figure 2.5.

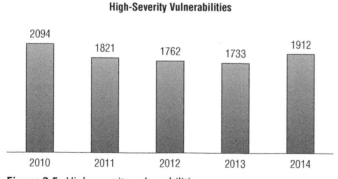

Figure 2.5: High-severity vulnerabilities

There is no shortage of vulnerabilities to gain access, and the evidence indicates the supply will continue. Yet there are different levels of initial access depending on who and what is compromised. In the physical world, a thief technically "has access" to a bank when they are standing in the lobby. This is very different than being alone inside the vault with keys to the safety deposit boxes after hours.

Likewise, initial access can vary from that of a restricted user on an unimportant computer to full access rights on a key piece of critical infrastructure. In the beginning, the Attacker will not be picky. Any access is better than none. This partially explains why, for example, there have been 70+ reported vulnerabilities in WordPress since 2010. The Attacker is unlikely to care about the information the popular website management and blogging software holds. It's probably already public. Compromising WordPress provides initial access to the web server, a toehold on the target's network. (The complete explanation is that it also gives the Attacker a way to serve up malware to others.)

Preventing this initial access is the focus of much of the security industry. Whether it's a good network design that limits the attack surface area, or an intrusion detection system that looks for known patterns of malicious network traffic, the industry has spent much of the past 2 decades trying to keep the Attacker out.

The results of this effort, unfortunately, speak for themselves. Attackers have found a way around almost every technology that seeks to prevent initial access, and once they do, they maintain that access for the long haul.

Stage 3: Persistence

Persistence is the art of turning initial access into reoccurring access. It is the foundation that makes sustaining an operation possible.

Persistence is the first defensive action of the Attacker, the consolidation and securing of future access. Vulnerabilities are unreliable. First, they are of unknown duration: some may last years, others a few weeks. Second, they do not always work. Depending on the type of vulnerability and the skill of the Attacker, success rates can vary from 1 in 10 to every time. Staking future access on a vulnerability is a poor plan.

Attackers must install their own form of persistence, commonly called a *backdoor*. The goal is to maintain access through normal usage, including system restarts, and to establish a reliable command and control channel.

Persistence can take many forms: an addition to the web browser, a new Run key entry, a modification to the computer's boot process, and more. The Microsoft tool Autoruns lists over 15 different methods of persisting on Windows. And those are just the approved ones.

Some methods require a user to login to become active. Others only require the computer to turn on. Regardless of form, persistence seeks to eliminate the need to ever have to repenetrate security again.

Personal security products have had varying degrees of success preventing the establishment of persistence on desktop computers. Most, for example, will catch and then prompt a user to confirm installing a *driver*—a privileged program that interacts with the underlying operating system.

This has caused Attackers to engage in an arms race; to redouble their efforts and find new ways to persist that are not monitored by these products; to attack the prevention methods directly; or to persist on routers, servers, or other computers that do not run personal security products. Regardless of who is winning at the moment, the persistence stage will remain a key battleground area between offense and defense.

Stage 4: Expansion

Expansion involves increasing access to a target network. This is done to establish a more robust level of persistence or to locate and access wanted data. The Stuxnet attack went after centrifuge controllers, but the initial access probably started on an unrelated computer and expanded.

Even in less advanced cases, expansion is a necessity. Companies commonly employ tiered network architectures like the sample shown in Figure 2.6.

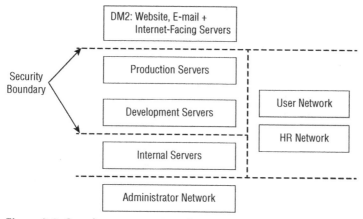

Figure 2.6: Sample corporate network

The Attacker must expand to persist. Initial access usually starts in the DMZ or on the user network. These segments are by far the most vulnerable to the outside world. However, they are also the most monitored. Beyond that, the Attacker will not want to have their access through a single point of failure. Maintaining access as the target network updates, upgrades, and expands itself is no small task.

In addition, the initial access point will rarely contain the communications, credit card databases, design drawings, or payroll data that the Attacker wants. The Attacker must expand to be successful. This information is located elsewhere, spread among different users, production servers, and internal file servers.

Expansion is time intensive. It requires surveying, collecting, and analyzing information to identify the next step of the operation. It can take months and sometimes years for an Attacker to go from her initial point of access to the virtual crown jewels.

It is also the stage of greatest Attacker susceptibility because it may require subverting internal security. For example, the Attacker may gain access to the Administrator network to bridge connectivity between parts of the company or to secure privileged credentials. Or, she may have an internal server push data to the DMZ for retrieval. These actions are not "normal" to the network.

Despite these potential anomalies, expansion is one area lacking in defensive technologies. Although products look at a specific computer's actions, to date, few, if any, can correlate anomalous actions across a network and present something actionable. Expansion is necessary, and therefore detecting it is an area for defensive improvement.

Stage 5: Exfiltration

Exfiltration is the retrieval of wanted data from the target network. There is no use in gaining access to a network if you cannot get data back out of it. Exfiltration is the ultimate measure of success for strategic and directed collection operations. Even non-kinetic CNA may have exfiltration requirements because an Attacker is going to want some sense of the amount of damage done to the network.

Initial access and expansion deal with establishing a command and control channel to the right portions of the target network. It is a different problem to retrieve large amounts of data. The Attacker must contend with the trade-off between the amount of data, the speed of retrieval, and operational security. The more data retrieved or the faster it is transmitted, the more noticeable it is.

From the Defender's perspective, exfiltration is a hard problem. When you exclude volume of data, it is difficult to differentiate legitimate outbound traffic from carefully crafted malicious traffic. There are simply countless ways to embed data going out of a network. Do your users e-mail outside contacts, use chat, post to facebook, or browse the web? If so, there is a way to exfiltrate data.

Without exfiltration there is no point to the operation, excluding the most contrived non-kinetic CNA scenarios. This stage, like others before, is performed continuously. It is and will remain a key battleground area between offense and defense.

Stage 6: Detection

Detection occurs when an operation is exposed to the target. Detection is like death: the exact timing is unknown; it may come suddenly or after a long decline.

Consider that the most sophisticated attacks known to date are just that, *known*. Attacks include

- Stuxnet—Targeting Iran's nuclear program
- Flamer—Targeting various Mideast countries

- Operation Aurora—Targeting Google, Adobe, Juniper, and others
- Red October—Targeting diplomatic and government agencies, particularly in Eastern Europe

Each of these operations is suspected to be backed by nation states with enormous resources. And yet, all of them were detected. It may have taken years, but they succumbed. When that detection occurred, years' worth of offensive technological development and thousands of hours invested into the operations evaporated. Hopefully for the Attacker, there were contingency plans in place to absorb this loss. Hopefully for those and other potential targets, there weren't.

Are there other undetected operations out there? Without question. But to ignore detection as a natural part of the operational life cycle is to condemn an Attacker to a perpetual series of crises. To quote Forrest Gump, "It happens." An Attacker must develop both their technical and nontechnical strategies accordingly.

Principle of Access

There is always someone with legitimate access and a means to use it.[5]

The first principle of access is the Attacker's comfort. As Duggan and Parks wrote almost 15 years ago, the virtual world is "built and controlled by humans and their tools." No matter the security in place, some person has access to whatever the Attacker is after. The Attacker's goal is therefore to find a method to subvert and assume the identity of a legitimate user or software agent with such access. This may be difficult, but it is never impossible.

If this were a movie, then gaining access to a high-value computer network would require an elaborate disguise, retina-altering contact lenses, and a set of cables to suspend the intruder above the pressure-sensitive floor. (Okay, did anyone else think about how the CIA could have saved millions of dollars on biometric locks and pressure-sensitive flooring by hooking up a $100 motion detector to a $5 air horn? I digress.) Outside the movies, impersonating a legitimate user is much less elaborate.

The approach the Attacker takes to gain initial access depends on the type of connectivity the target network offers. There are four basic types of connectivity: inbound access, outbound access, both, and neither. Each type presents a different type of challenge to overcome.

Inbound Access

A network that enables inbound access means that someone from outside the network can initiate a connection into the network as shown in Figure 2.7.

Inbound Access

Figure 2.7: Network with inbound access

Inbound access can be open to everyone, like a public website, or restricted. When restricted, access is controlled by one or more of the following: something one knows, something one has, or the virtual location.

The "know" part is typically a password; though it may also be a VPN key, a picture selection, or a specific mouse movement, among other things. The user connects, is prompted to enter a password or perform some kind of action, and access is granted.

The "have" part is a physical item, such as a secure key fob or a cell phone. The user confirms possession of the item by sending information that only the item's possessor could have, such as a random confirmation code sent via a text message to the phone.

The "virtual location" of access control limits connections to those originating from specifically allowed network addresses. Unless the user initiates the connection from a specific point, the connection will be denied. This method of access control is meant to limit the avenues of attack.

Each of these forms of access control is subject to attack. Passwords, or any form of knowledge, can be guessed or stolen. Hardware tokens can be stolen or reverse engineered. The latter was done in March 2011, when someone hacked RSA, the provider of SecureID tokens for two-factor authentication, and then used this information to break into several U.S. defense contractors.

Cell phones can be stolen or infected with malware. A malicious program for smart phones dubbed Zeus-in-the-mobile, or ZitMo, intercepts banking codes known as mobile transaction authentication numbers (mTAN) and forwards them to the Attacker. This allows the Attacker to gain the access necessary to initiate banking transactions without physical access to the victim's phone.

Finally, controlling by virtual location just moves the line of defense one hop out. Defense becomes as effective as that next network. When Attackers learn the allowed points of origin, they will gain access by compromising those networks first.

The previous attack methods work by impersonating *legitimate* access. There are also methods of gaining illegitimate access. The Attacker may circumvent all access control by exploiting an exposed software service. This is done by taking advantage of a logic or programming flaw in a software program that is accessible by outsiders. The famed Morris Worm, which allegedly took down some 10 percent of the Internet in 1988, spread by this method.

Illegitimate access can also be gained by escalating privileges. This means the Attacker leverages regular user-level access, such as that provided by Facebook, Netflix, or thousands of other companies, to gain more access or gather more information than the company intended to grant. The social media texting and photo-sharing application Snapchat fell victim to this kind of attack when someone managed to leverage a regular user account to gather the account information of millions of other users.

In short, allowing any kind of inbound access increases the target's susceptibility. In addition, attacks can be waged on the Attacker's time frame. Most inbound access is open 24 hours per day, 7 days a week. The Attacker can hammer away at finding inbound flaws around the clock.

Yet there are no easy answers. Denying all access may deny a company's employees the flexibility of working from home. It may stop a headquarters IT person from fixing issues in a satellite office. It may prevent communication with vendors or customers. In some cases, like the aforementioned Snapchat, having users that can access inbound services is what makes their business a business.

Denying all inbound access is not realistic. The Attacker knows this and will look for ways to impersonate legitimate access or grant themselves illegitimate access.

Outbound Access

A network that allows outbound access means that someone from inside the network can initiate a connection to somewhere outside the network as shown in Figure 2.8. If someone can browse the web, then the network allows outbound access. Most networks do.

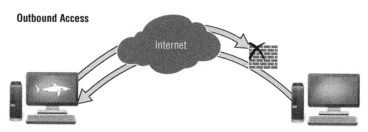

Figure 2.8: Network with outbound access

How does the Attacker go after a network when there is nothing accessible from the outside to attack? Simple. They get the user to do something that connects out to them. This often begins with an e-mail.

E-mail Attacks

E-mail is a common approach to attacking a network with outbound connectivity. There are three basic approaches to an e-mail attack: attachments, attacking the e-mail program, and malicious links.

The first generation of malicious e-mail attachments was to attach an executable program to an e-mail and ask the user to execute it—simple, direct, and for a long time, effective. The attached program might pretend to do something useful such as play a video or extract compressed files, or it may appear to do nothing at all, but in the background, it would install something to grant access to the Attacker. This blatant approach still works now and again, but automatic filtering and user awareness has cut down on its effectiveness.

The second generation of e-mail attachments were not programs, but documents that contained the ability to run code. Most notably, the Microsoft Office product line offered a "macro" feature by which people could script certain behavior within a document, such as inserting the current date or restricting a field to numbers only. The macros had few restrictions. They could, for example, access the e-mail program Microsoft Outlook and send a copy of the document to the first 50 e-mail addresses in the address book. This is what the Melissa Virus did in 1999 to infect hundreds of thousands of computers. Microsoft has since instituted macro security to prevent this kind of blatant behavior.

The third generation of e-mail attachments were programs again, but they didn't seem to be programs. Files with esoteric extensions such as .chm or .hta would slip through the filters and be run by users. The so-called iLOVEYOU virus spread as LOVE-LETTER-FOR-YOU.txt.vbs, and Microsoft Windows by default would helpfully hide the .vbs part of the file and make it look like a harmless text file. E-mail filters have since been updated to catch most of these; though occasionally something slips through.

The final and current generation of e-mail attachments takes advantage of the programs that open them. These attachments are Microsoft Word documents (.doc), Excel spreadsheets (.xls), Adobe PDFs (.pdf), compressed files (.zip), or other third-party application-specific documents. When these poisoned documents are opened, they exploit vulnerabilities within the applications themselves to execute Attacker-supplied code. Go check the spam folder on a Yahoo, Hotmail, and Gmail account to find a recent example.

The next e-mail-based attack approach is to send a specially crafted e-mail that corrupts the e-mail program into executing Attacker-supplied code. This is the ideal attack because it requires nothing more from the user than previewing or viewing the e-mail. The extra step of opening an attachment is not necessary. These types of attacks were quite common in the early days of Microsoft Outlook and Outlook Express. Though they have waned, they still crop up now again against Outlook, Lotus Notes, or other popular corporate e-mail clients.

The last e-mail-based attack approach is to send a link to a website. Most users have heard the admonition against opening attachments, but what is so harmful about a link? People browse the web and go to random websites all the time. This is exactly the point. Because of conditioning, a link seems much less dangerous.

However, these links bring the user to websites that are specifically designed to leverage vulnerabilities in web browsers or their plug-ins. Internet Explorer, Firefox, Safari, Chrome, and other less popular browsers have all had numerous vulnerabilities in which just visiting a website is enough to give the website operator control of the client computer. And even if these web browsers were perfect, which history shows otherwise, there are myriad plug-ins that have an even worse track record. Active X, Flash, and Java are often used to make websites seem more interactive, and they have been a historical death knell to browser security. Links are just as unsafe as attachments.

Again, there are no easy answers. Opening e-mails from only those people you know isn't practical for most businesses, and even if it were, it isn't much protection. E-mail is easily spoofed. Beyond that, the sender may be compromised. Virus after virus has made use of people's e-mail address books to spread themselves in a more convincing manner.

E-mail attacks are executed with the goal of gaining a foothold on the network. After that foothold is gained, the Attacker can circumvent outbound restrictions as explained in "Circumventing Outbound Restrictions" later in the section.

Website Hijack Attacks

Using e-mail is not the only way to gain a foothold on the network that only allows outbound access. Another approach is to commandeer legitimate sites that the Attacker knows or hopes a target user will visit. These have been dubbed "watering hole" attacks because the Attacker waits for the target to come to them. This has the same result as an e-mail link–based attack except it does not require the e-mail to direct the user.

There are a few ways of commandeering a site. The first, and most obvious, is for the Attacker to take over and replace the content of a popular website with malicious code. Generally, the Attacker inserts a small amount of code into the existing website so that nothing appears amiss to the user.

The second approach is to use a cross-site-scripting attack (XSS). In the more dangerous form of this kind of attack, the Attacker uploads code that the website then displays to other users—any site that allows users to post information or comments, such as Monster.com, is potentially vulnerable. You may think you are just viewing the profile of John Smith, when in reality, John's online resume contains malicious code that attacks your browser directly or redirects you to another site that does. As the target, you are visiting a legitimate site, and yet you may still be compromised. Ebay, LinkedIn, Facebook Chat, Twitter, the NYTimes, and countless other household-name websites have had cross-site-scripting vulnerabilities.

A third approach avoids commandeering the website itself, but instead hijacks the domain name. The domain name system, or DNS, allows users to find and connect to computers by name instead of by the more esoteric IP address. Every website, for example www.example.com, registers its name with a domain name registrar, which responds to queries about where the computer with that name is located. Browse to www.example.com, and behind the scenes, your computer will query a DNS server, get a response of 93.184.216.119 (as of this writing), and then connect to that address.

The registrars are vulnerable to being hacked or tricked into changing this information. When this happens, and you browse to www.example.com, your browser will be redirected to somewhere else entirely. In 2013, a group hijacked the security company Rapid7's website in this manner by sending a spoofed fax to Rapid7's registrar, Register.com. This particular case was immediately obvious as the group defaced the site with a political message, but other examples have been more subtle and served up malicious software.

Finally, commandeering a website may not even be necessary. Ad networks serve up advertisements that can be placed by anyone, including the Attacker, across a wide range of websites. Most advertising companies attempt to sanitize malicious code from the ads before displaying them, but they are not always successful.

There are also many shady malware serving websites and a plethora of "free" software that is tainted and posted for download. Many of these websites are intertwined with pornography, illegal software, or pirated movies, all things that human nature seems to seek out. Name any company over 1,000 employees, and odds are there will be at least one employee there that has used a company computer to browse these parts of the Internet while at work, opening the company up to an intrusion.

Website hijacking attacks have one goal in common: to provide a method of attacking a network that allows only outbound connections. There are many different ways to accomplish this task, but all are a type of positional access operation designed to lead one step closer to the target.

Other Attacks

There are still more ways to go after a network that allows only outbound access. Someone could spread malicious thumb drives in the parking lot. In 2011, the Department of Homeland Security performed this exact test against several federal agencies and contractors. Roughly 60 percent of CDs and thumb drives picked up were inserted into a computer; 90 percent if they contained an official logo; and it only takes one instance to breach security.[5]

Or give thumb drives out as part of a gift basket as the Russians did for diplomats at a G20 meeting. You know what they say "Beware of Russians bearing removable media."

The Attacker may look for employees with company laptops. If people connect the laptop to both their home network and the corporate network, the corporate network is only as secure as their home network.

The Attacker may also look for wireless access points they can reach. Does the company share an office building with someone else? Then someone else can likely sit unwatched and attempt to penetrate the wireless network for hours on end.

Speaking of wireless, smartphones have provided an entirely new vector. If a person is allowed to bring their phone into work and connect it to the company wireless network, there's another attack vector to gain access from the inside.

Certainly there are even more technical methods.

On the nontechnical side, there is just plain calling people and asking them to do something that compromises their security. This is called social engineering, and as Kevin Mitnick famously detailed through his escapades compromising the security of PacBell and other organizations, it is quite effective.

There are also physical access attacks such as breaking in and installing hardware or software, getting a job at the target, or by paying off an insider. These require a geographically colocated Attacker, a hurdle to be sure, but they are possible.

Between e-mail, website hijacks, and other attacks, the Attacker has many different possible ways to gain initial access to a network that only allows outbound connections.

Circumventing Outbound Restrictions

All the preceding methods can gain the Attacker access to a single computer on the network, but it still doesn't solve the problem of how to communicate with that computer. The network may allow outbound access, but that access may be restricted.

The first way to restrict access is through software running on the host computer, such as parental control software. This type of software monitors all outbound connections and either allows them, blocks them, or prompts the user asking what to do. Personal security products, such as Kaspersky Internet Security or McAffee Internet Security, use this method. "XYZ process is trying to connect to `www.example.com`. Do you wish to allow?"

The Attacker might rely on the user to click "Allow." Or they may attack the host-based software directly and attempt to prevent that message from ever appearing. All host-based software has a way to override it if a person has full system access. It must. At a minimum, the program must have a way to be uninstalled.

Early versions of personal security products did a poor job of preventing local users from overriding their settings. Access lists were unencrypted and could be modified to add malicious software. User prompts could be closed directly by the malicious program by spoofing mouse clicks. But companies learned their lesson and now host-based security programs such as McAfee, Kaspersky, and Symantec guard against this weakness and do all sorts of things to prevent users, even privileged users, from easily disabling their software. Ultimately, this just leads to an ongoing war of attrition in which, at any given moment, one side is winning.

The second way to restrict access is through software or hardware on the network, such as a firewall or proxy server. A firewall allows or denies network traffic based on a set of criteria such as the type of traffic or the destination. A proxy serves as an intermediary between a computer and the desired network destination.

Altering or overriding network restrictions is not as straightforward as attacking host-based software. The Attacker must gain access to the network device itself. Given the diversity of network layout and types of devices, doing this "blind," that is, with preprogrammed software, is difficult.

Therefore, to circumvent these network devices, the Attacker generally needs to establish a command and control channel into the network to make intelligent decisions. Establishing this channel, however, requires circumventing the network device first. Chicken, meet egg.

Rather than confront the problem, the Attacker avoids it by establishing outbound connections via allowed network protocols, that is, e-mail, Facebook message, instant message, and so on. This reduces the problem from attacking network devices to just determining what type of network traffic is allowed out. And this is a much easier problem.

Outbound network restrictions are notoriously porous because strict policies tend to get in the way of business. Try blocking all outbound web traffic, and what happens to the HR employee trying to research state law or search resume sites? The same thing that happens to the marketing employee researching the competition. Their work stops. This bias toward actually getting work done weakens outbound restrictions considerably.

Of course, it may seem that if the Attacker is trying to connect out of the network, they already have access. This is one-half true. The Attacker may gain initial access from a Trojan e-mail attachment or any of the methods previously mentioned, but until communication is established, the Attacker does not yet have repeatable access. In a network that allows outbound access only, the Attacker's challenge is to leverage this initial software execution to circumvent host-based and network-based restrictions and establish command and control.

Bidirectional Access

Bidirectional access, as shown in Figure 2.9, is the norm for most networks. Some types of connections are allowed in and others allowed out. Each direction may have its own set of access controls, restrictions, and monitoring.

Figure 2.9: Network with bidirectional access

   A more complicated network will also be segmented where specific parts of it are allowed to connect in or out in certain ways. Inbound access may be allowed to the company website but nowhere else. Users in the IT group may be allowed to use the file transfer protocol (FTP) to download data, but users on the regular user segment of the network are blocked.
   The Attacker approaches a bidirectional network following the path of least resistance. Perhaps they gain initial execution via a website hijacking attack, but then they use that to open an inbound path. The Attacker mixes and matches approaches for the greatest effect.

No Outside Access

A network with no outside connectivity is commonly called an isolated network or an "air-gapped" network. (The term *air-gapped* was invented before wireless networks.) This network is physically separated from the Internet as shown in Figure 2.10. Access is controlled first and foremost by physical presence: the gates, guards, and locks of the buildings in which it is housed.

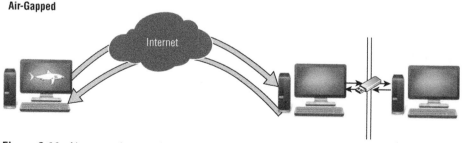

Figure 2.10: Air-gapped network

An air-gapped network takes the security versus convenience trade-off to the extreme. It is the most secure network configuration possible to protect against outsider threats and the most inconvenient for sharing information or administering.

Most secure, though, does not mean invulnerable. It just raises the bar. To gain access, the Attacker must breach physical security or trick, cajole, bribe, or blackmail users into doing it for them. A few theoretical examples of this have been covered: thumb drives in the parking lot, compromising phones or laptops that are moved into and out of the network. But there are also real-world examples.

Kevin Mitnick exploited physical security and gained access to telecommunication systems by dressing as a telephone repairman and using the right jargon and other social engineering tactics. The networks may not have been air-gapped, but they could have been. It would not have mattered. He gained access without breaking a single lock or disabling a single alarm.

In 2010, an air gap did not prevent the Stuxnet worm from compromising the stand-alone network at Iranian nuclear facilities. The method of Stuxnet's introduction is unknown and likely to stay that way, but it is possible the person was an "unwitting" insider threat, someone who moved data to the network but did not realize it contained a threat.

And, of course, there are perfectly "witting" insider threats. In 2013, an air gap (presumably) did not prevent Edward Snowden from taking an untold number of classified documents from the National Security Agency and handing them to the press. Again, the network may or may not have been isolated, but it doesn't matter; the attack would have worked just the same.

For an air-gapped network, the Attacker must find a way to be, to corrupt, or to compromise an insider. When achieved, this reduces the problem of physical access to one of insider threat security, a much easier problem.

Access Summary

Someone has legitimate access to each thing the Attacker wants. The Attacker's challenge is therefore to either circumvent any access controls, or impersonate or corrupt someone that is allowed through. Exactly how this is approached will change depending on the nature of the network. Regardless, the first principle of access means that though this task can be made extremely difficult, it is always possible. All security systems have a weakness, the legitimate users, and these people are exploitable.

Principle of Economy

Ambitions will always exceed available resources.

All ambitions are tempered by the constraints of reality. Whether it is finding targets, exfiltrating more data, or improving one's position on a network, there is always more that could be done and not enough resources to do it. Understanding these constraints is paramount in building an offensive framework.

The types of resource constraints are constant across different operations; though which resource is in shortest supply will vary greatly from day to day and from operation to operation.

Time

Time is required to conduct all stages of an operation. And it is critical for most every objective. Finding out about a drug shipment 2 months too late is not particularly useful if the goal was to intercept it.

There is only so much time the Attacker can spend on any specific target or on any one aspect of an operation. Time limits the development of offensive capabilities and the accumulation of expertise. It eats away at existing capabilities and makes technical knowledge stale. Time affects the development and use of all other resources and is therefore the most important constraint.

Targeting Capabilities

Targeting is often the most difficult and expensive part of an operation. It may require all source intelligence that collectively identifies information about a country's political, economic, or military structure. Though much is available on the Internet, much is not. In some cases, it may require the intelligence resources of a nation-state to gather.

But gathering this kind of information is not the only skill required. When gathered, targeting may require linguists, analysts, technical expertise, and subject matter experts in the target's field. For example, if Attackers want to steal from a Saudi Arabian bank, they likely need fluency in Arabic and detailed knowledge of how financial transactions work, even if they already have full access to the bank's network.

Assembling, maintaining, and training an effective team with all these varied skillsets is nontrivial and places a limitation on the Attacker's overall operational abilities.

Exploitation Expertise

Exploitation is the ability to find and exploit vulnerabilities in software programs, hardware devices, or network configurations. This expertise is required during initial access, persistence, and expansion. Without exploitation expertise, the Attacker cannot perform even the most basic operation.

Exploitation expertise requires detailed low-level knowledge of programming languages, operating systems, and hardware. It requires understanding compilers, memory managers, program data structures, and more. The practiced exploitation engineer needs the ability, patience, and mind-set to reverse engineer programs and devices to extract the most minute details and then manipulate them to his advantage.

Few of the technical skills necessary to find and develop vulnerabilities into real-world exploits are taught in the typical college curriculum. A security course may teach what a buffer overflow is and how to avoid creating one, but there is questionable academic value in teaching the intricacies of how it can be exploited to compromise a computer. Academic programs that do are the exception. Therefore, the exploitation skillset must be learned outside of standard programs, making it hard to find and expensive to cultivate.

Of course, there is no shortage of publicly available exploits that the Attacker can download and use. Money can also help mitigate the problem as exploits are routinely sold on gray and black markets for anywhere from thousands to hundreds of thousands of dollars. Yet regardless of whether the exploitation expertise is in-house, copied, donated, or purchased, it is a valuable resource necessary for all operations.

Networking Expertise

Networking expertise is the in-depth understanding of the myriad technologies used to build, operate, manage, and monitor a computer network. It is required throughout an operation, but most important during initial access, expansion, and exfiltration.

Now, generally Attackers do not have the benefit of network diagrams and configurations to guide them through. From the moment of initial access, Attackers are in the middle of a fog. While initially ignorant to their surroundings, they have to find a way to safely establish communication, to persist, to expand, to traverse, and to search a network, all while remaining hidden. (One of the objects of their search will certainly be for networking diagrams to make all this easier.)

These tasks require a thorough understanding of networks. Target networks can range from a few devices connected together via a single switch to thousands of computers and hundreds of switches that span continents. The technology involved can span decades, from old decrepit mainframes to the shiniest new application servers. In spite of this variety, Attackers must quickly gain their bearings and act.

Networking expertise creates the ability to envision plausible layouts, configurations, policies, and potential traps from little information. It is essential to exploiting a network efficiently.

Software Development Expertise

Software development expertise is the ability to develop, debug, maintain, expand, and test quality custom-built software. It is required to create robust attack, data collection, and analysis tools that are essential to all elements of the operational life cycle.

In most respects, software for CNE is no different than any other software project. However, additional constraints are placed on the CNE software engineer that are unusual to typical commercial software.

Foremost, CNE software must be fault tolerant to the extreme. Telling the "user," that is, the target, to reboot and try again is not an option. The software used during initial access, for example, cannot report any form of success or failure unless the core of the program itself is successful. This is another chicken-and-egg problem that can be addressed only by writing software that rarely fails.

CNE software must also be highly efficient and consume few computing resources or bandwidth. There is no displaying an hour glass or spinning wheel to indicate the computer may be slow for a moment while a task completes. The slightest hiccup in performance could push a user to investigate.

CNE software often explicitly breaks or circumvents operating system and program norms. This makes it extremely sensitive to minute variations in the target environment, an environment the Attacker has no control over and little foreknowledge of. This raises the bar substantially for testing because even something as little as the current level of memory usage can affect some tools.

Finally, and perhaps the biggest difference, CNE software must work even though other programs are specifically designed to counter it. Though commercial software developers may deal with incompatibilities, none are worried about software that is specifically designed to seek out and destroy it. Okay, that is an overstatement. Defensive security vendors deal with the same problem, as do the engineers that create software licensing systems. These software development efforts are directly attacked by the CNE and pirating communities, respectively. Regardless, withstanding direct attacks is a different kind of mind-set that requires cultivation.

Altogether, a specialized and often-constrained form of software development expertise is required to create the tools used in all aspects of an operation. Without it, operational capabilities will stagnate and through time become completely ineffective.

Operational Expertise

Operational expertise is essential to creatively sustaining operations in the face of adversity. If operations were simple and experience without value, then Attackers would have long ago completely automated the process. (The easier parts have in fact already been automated.)

Rather, operations are complicated and require active decisions ranging from the trivial to the transformative. The most important of these decisions is what to do when things go wrong, when the software fails, when the network is not laid out as believed, and when the proverbial plan falls part. The collection software failed, and there's no indication why. Was it found and removed? Is there some incompatibility that was never tested? Should it be restarted? There is no easy template for answering these types of questions. Experience is required.

Attackers with operational expertise can adapt existing or improvise new techniques to accomplish their operational objective while remaining undetected. Like exploitation expertise, this skill is not taught in a standard IT program. It must be learned through real-world experience.

Operational Analysis Expertise

Operational analysis is leveraged to direct each step and every movement of the Attacker in every stage of the life cycle. Operational analysis may range from diagraming the network, identifying users, searching through collected data, translating documents, or aiding in the selection of tools to manage the Attacker's profile.

Depending on the operation, operational analysts may have a total lack of information or complete overload. They must not only analyze the information they have, but also determine what they are lacking. Analysts must synthesize information from disparate sources across disciplines to answer urgent questions.

For example, an operational question might be, "If and when will the target upgrade?" This simple question is crucial for sustaining an operation. Answering it may require understanding the target's finances, their access to new equipment, their update history, or even the temperament of the system administrators. This is not a simple task.

Operational analysts require years of both technical and nontechnical experience to be effective, and like the other skillsets mentioned, it is not taught.

Technical Resources

Technical resources include those things necessary to conduct operations. Examples include infrastructure, bandwidth, software, and more.

Some technical resource issues can be addressed with money. If Attackers need more bandwidth, they can buy more bandwidth. More computers (depending on the country) are just a click and a shipment away.

Others resource issues, however, may have no readily available solution. For example, a target may use proprietary technology that is hard to acquire for analysis. Do you know what a 40-year-old power plant in Turkmenistan uses to control internal processes? I don't. But whatever it is, I doubt it can be ordered on Amazon.com. This target-imposed technical constraint is not easily overcome.

Yet of all the constraints of economy, technical resources are of the least concern. Smart, capable, and creative Attackers with enough time and money will undoubtedly find a way around any technical resource constraint.

Economy Summary

Attacker ambitions will inevitably exceed available resources. This is especially true because attacking requires specialized skill sets and experience not commonly taught. Talent is the key economic concern of any Attacker, regardless of resource level or structure.

Attacker Structure

There's a saying in the design of modern architecture that "form follows function." This tenet, first put forth in a poem by Louis H. Sullivan, means that the structure of a building, an organization, indeed "of all things physical and metaphysical, of all things human" comes from its purpose.

The technical purpose of the Attacker is to move through the operational life cycle and exfiltrate information while avoiding detection. If we assume the Attacker is flexible and efficient, we can infer a form or structure from the purpose.

Each stage of the operation requires different, though sometimes overlapping, technical and operational skillsets to execute. A human and economical approach would be to split these skillsets and corresponding functions into operating units.

Evidence for this approach is shown in the findings of Operation SMN, "a coordinated effort amongst leading private-industry security companies, led by Novetta,"[6] in its analysis of the so-called Axiom Attacker, suspected to be part of Chinese intelligence.

We also assess that different groups associated with the Axiom threat actor group likely perform various phases. This deduction is supported by the number of differences in the observed activity during these compromise stages which suggest a number of separate teams with varying responsibilities during their operation lifecycle... [D]ifferences in command and control (C2) and midpoint proxy infrastructure displayed... have led us to believe that the operational tempo, security policies, and acceptable risk levels are drastically different.[6]

So what might these groups be? Again, The operational life cycle consists of targeting, initial access, persistence, expansion, and exfiltration. And these require targeting, exploitation, networking, and other areas of expertise laid out in the "Economy" section of this chapter.

With this knowledge, we can postulate what a working structure for Axiom might be:

- Targeting—The driver of the overall operation. They are the high-level team that ultimately gives the orders for what to go after. They are steeped in the technical, political, or other importance of the target.

- Door kicking team—The driver of initial access. Their mission is to get in and establish communications. This team comprises or is supported by a general-purpose vulnerability discovery team and a tactical vulnerability discovery team for finding cross-target vulnerabilities and target-specific vulnerabilities, respectively.

- Rapid analysis team—The driver of persistence and immediate expansion. Their mission is to find out as much as they can as quickly as possible and establish redundant command and control. This team comprises or is supported by a tactical software development team capable of creating the customized solutions Axiom deployed.

- Networking team—The driver of long-term expansion and exfiltration. Their mission is to creep through the network and attain an ever-higher level of access while finding the optimal methods of exfiltrating data. This team comprises or is supported by networking engineers and a general-purpose software development team.

- Maintenance team—The driver of sustaining the operation. Their mission is to keep abreast of changes in target network layout or security posture while continuing to burrow ever deeper and steal ever more.

- Infrastructure team—The driver of finding, compromising, and maintaining viable website or e-mail domain attack vectors, command and control infrastructure, and often transient exfiltration points. This team may be supported by the same vulnerability specialists used in the rapid analysis team.

In total, this is six separate functional teams with up to four support teams.

Is this truly how Axiom is structured? We can only make an educated guess. Perhaps some operational functions are shared within a single team or others are further subdivided. Perhaps they have smaller multidisciplinary attack teams, more like a Special Forces unit.

In the end, the specific structure is irrelevant as it will be different between different Attackers. But understanding the general structure that Axiom requires to perform operations leads to some conclusions:

- Attackers are composed of specialists with depth of skill.
- Coordinating specialties requires some level of organizational complexity.
- The communication between units is a potential weak point. Given the Attacker is human, the different tempos, risk tolerances, tools, expertise, and leadership of the units will inevitably lead to miscommunication and potential mistakes.

Finally, the professionalism of a group like Axiom requires a strategy to build, manage, and lead. The defense will require a similar level of depth, coordination, and strategy, a bigger well-directed boat as it were, to avoid getting eaten alive.

Summary

Attackers are human, and this humanity drives the objective and nature of operations. Within those operations, there will always be a way for Attackers to gain access, whether remotely or by compromising an insider. Always. However, the ability of Attackers to find or leverage this potential access is limited by economic constraints. Together these first principles of humanity, access, and economy underlie all aspects of Attackers, their structure and their actions.

In the next chapter, we'll investigate how these same first principles impact the defense.

The Defender

I really didn't foresee the Internet. But then, neither did the computer industry. Not that that tells us very much of course—the computer industry didn't even foresee that the century was going to end.

—Douglas Adams, author, *The Hitchhiker's Guide to the Galaxy*

The defense is routinely overworked and outgunned. If you lock the doors to your home, you may feel safe against potential thieves, but you also know that those locks won't keep out an army squad backed by a battalion. Nor are you particularly concerned about that kind of military threat, at least not in the United States. Yet, in terms of resources, that is exactly what a network defense is up against: a well-trained group of 7 to 10 individuals directly supported by hundreds, and indirectly supported by thousands.

It's not a fair fight, but is it more than just numbers? Answering this requires understanding the nature of defense. And just like the Attacker, the defense is guided and restricted by the principles of CNE.

Principle of Humanity

I have used the word *target* liberally to refer to the targeted network, data, or the people administering and using that network, but the Defender has no such ambiguity. The *Defender* consists solely of the people actively or passively preventing the Attacker from completing any portion of the operational life cycle. (As with the Attacker, the Defender warrants a proper noun to emphasize the human element.)

Some aspects of the defense are human themselves: the users, administrators, and creators of the technology deployed. Clearly, people have all the strengths and weaknesses of, well, people. Yet humanity bleeds into the technical aspects of defense as well. Two such examples of importance to an Attacker are network layout and technical security policy.

Humanity and Network Layout

Understanding the layout of a network is essential for the Attacker to efficiently exploit it. So how "human" could a network layout possibly be? When you think of a computer network, the first word that comes to mind is usually not "personality." (Unless, of course, it is paired with the word "temperamental," but that's another issue.) Yet, networks have one human trait: they grow organically.

Networks do not start out with thousands of centrally managed computers and networking devices all wired together and switched on in concert. Some companies start with a handful of computers and stay that way. Others expand. Still others are large companies that existed before the computer revolution and have installed, integrated, and upgraded the technology piecemeal. Some are amalgamations thrown together by the takeovers, mergers, and reorganizations that companies routinely withstand. Few companies of any reasonable size ever undergo clean network redesigns. And those that do are not rolled out all at once.

As an organization expands, the networks expand. As it acquires, the two (probably incompatible) networks will be connected through only a few connection points until such time as they can be integrated. Perhaps everything is cleanly integrated into a managed hierarchy like an Active Directory domain, tree, or forest (note the organic language). Or perhaps the integration never occurs and each part remains segmented.

As an organization contracts, it will leave unused, or at least underused, systems running. It takes much more effort to ferret out what is still in use than it does to just leave it in place. Throughout these changes, the human inertia of "if it ain't broke, don't fix it" often prevents any reconsideration of security. Show me a detailed network diagram, and like the rings of a tree, you can extract how the organization grew.

The technology choices of the network also mirror the history of an organization. If a company was set up before 1998, then it's probably running Microsoft Windows on the desktop. Why? Because that was the only scalable solution in existence at the time, and migrating to something new takes a lot more effort than upgrading. If it's a university, then it's probably running some form of UNIX (Linux, Solaris, and so forth) for its core infrastructure because that is what the scientific community used first.

The layout and technology of a network reflects an organization's business goals, its funding, and priorities. Because each of these influences is human in nature, the network itself will have an inherent humanity.

Humanity and Security Policy

The ideal system administrator is driven by a desire to create and maintain a well-functioning technological ecosystem that enables the productivity of the organization. That reads like a great job description, doesn't it? In reality, the administrator's motivation is to keep things working well enough that no one complains; improve them when necessary; and most important, keep the management happy.

Whether enforcing security restrictions falls under any of those categories depends greatly on the culture of the organization. Businesses that consider security essential to their core business will do so. Most do not. Many say security is important but do not invest the time and money to back it up.

However, let's say for the sake of argument that a business is security conscious. How are security restrictions enforced? Certainly there are physical and technical restrictions that prevent some actions—an office is locked or a file server is configured with access permissions. But many undesired behaviors cannot be explicitly prevented: a key can be shared, a safe left unlocked, or a single password could be shared by an office. How are these restrictions enforced? By policy, monitoring, and fear of consequences. This is true of any business asset whether it is the copy machine, the telephone, or the Internet.

How effective is policy? It depends. Policies are ignored if they are perceived as dumb. Blocking personal e-mail, for example, may be good security, but if users view it as "Why can't management just trust me to do my job?" then it quickly breeds resentment. Any blocks will be circumvented by some soon enough.

Willingness to ignore policy is a clear risk/reward trade-off that depends on the likelihood of getting caught and the consequences. How many people in your company have been fired for not following computer security policy? Answer: none. Perhaps someone has been fired for downloading pornography or for watching movies on the job, but those terminations were for legal and performance reasons, not security.

The problem with severe penalties is it is simply too easy to make an honest mistake to warrant such a regime. And even for intentional acts, drawing lines between behaviors is hard. Checking e-mail is relatively safe, but following links in e-mail is not. How does one enforce the difference? By firing the first person who follows a link to a newsletter from his kid's school? See how that goes.

A common refrain in the security industry has been to blame the user for ignoring good policy. Users do dumb security things: they open e-mail attachments, they reuse passwords across different systems, they bring documents in from home to print, and so on. This is true even when explicitly told not to.

Yet, these actions are entirely rational when viewed through the lens of humanity. Often users do not understand the reasons behind a rule and rarely are there consequences. The security consequences are at best vague, and the business consequences are nonexistent. Meanwhile, multiple passwords are difficult to remember. E-mail attachments are sent and received all the time, and users are conditioned to open them. Click Yes to allow an update to the system? Certainly if it makes the dialog box go away. Even the IT staff is not immune from these human considerations.

Security policy is irrelevant if not enforced through technical means or with severe consequences. Otherwise, all the policy in the world is not going to change behavior. The humanity of convenience and habit will always trump security policy.

Humanity Summary

The Defender is human, and even the technical elements will reflect that humanity. The Attacker understands this and will use it to their advantage to guess at network architectures, to circumvent security policy, to gain access, to hide, and to sustain their operation. The Defender must design security knowing it will be run by people with all their strengths and failings.

Principle of Access

Where the first principle of access is the Attacker's comfort, it is the Defender's daily struggle. The Defender must continue to provide access to legitimate users through technology updates, hardware and software failures, and network changes, all while keeping out the Attacker.

To do this, the Defender attempts to enforce the so-called Principle of Least Privilege, to limit access to documents, databases, and other resources to only those people who require them. It's a great ideal to strive for. The problem is in the implementation and its inherent feedback imbalance.

When access is mistakenly denied to a legitimate user, the user notices. Users complain when their e-mail breaks or they cannot generate some report or locate some document. The wheel squeaks when it has problems.

However, there is no such feedback for when access is mistakenly granted. The user may not even notice, much less complain. Every mistake in configuration, dormant account, or imperfect permission that leaves things too open has the potential to go unfixed for a long time.

And no one actually monitors access effectively. Chelsea Manning, formerly PFC Bradley Manning, downloaded hundreds of thousands of U.S. diplomatic cables and classified army reports onto a CD he labeled "Lady Gaga" without attracting the least bit of attention.[1] That's some poker face.

Meanwhile, Edward Snowden stole thousands of classified documents from the U.S. National Security Agency, though in his case, he reportedly used other people's credentials. Still, he copied all this data to thumb drives in an organization that supposedly restricts and monitors thumb drive access.[2]

Employing the Principle of Least Privilege is hard, even for organizations with high incentives to be secure. It requires seeking out feedback via the constant testing of security boundaries and the monitoring of access. By contrast, feedback for ensuring access just requires having an active user base.

From the Attacker point of view, the Defender is defined by the access that must be granted. The Defender may employ a variety of technical security measures to limit that access: firewalls that prevent connections, intrusion detection devices that search for malware, antivirus or personal security products that look for heuristic behavior; but any technical countermeasure must have a legitimate bypass. The first principle of access guarantees the Defender will always be vulnerable.

The Defensive Life Cycle

Before considering the principle of economy, take a brief detour into a typical cycle of defending against attacks. Offensive operations have a well-defined life cycle, but there is nothing so formal for the Defender. In fact, the Defender can choose to do nothing, as many do.

In response, many in the security community have offered versions of an ideal defensive life cycle. These are typically composed of stages such as assessment, implementation, testing, policy enforcement, penetration testing, and so forth. They are often a valid prescription of what to do, but not why: tactics without the strategy.

A strategic defensive life cycle (Figure 3.1) should examine how one actively counters the offensive life cycle. This creates an offensive death cycle as it were, in which each phase of an offensive operation meets a counterphase.

The offensive death cycle is composed of privacy, prevention, constraint, obstruction, detection, and response.

Privacy is the management of the publishing of information used for targeting: news group postings, org charts, partnership agreements, and such. Unfortunately, much of this information includes things that marketing may want to tout.

For example, defense contractor Lockheed Martin's cloud-based offering is based on Cisco, NetApp, and VMware technologies. Meanwhile, last year it established a partnership for security with Red Hat, Splunk, and FireEye. How do I know? Lockheed Martin press releases. Thanks to marketing, it took only 30 seconds to build a general list of technologies to exploit or avoid. Privacy is difficult to manage but, if done right, can be an important counter to targeting.

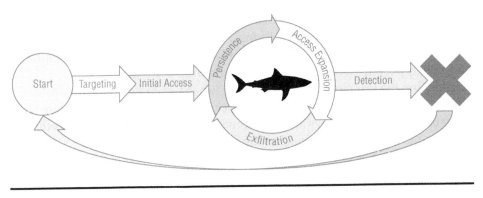

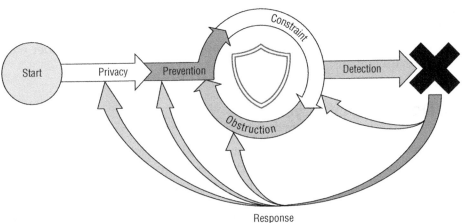

Figure 3.1: Strategic Defensive Life Cycle counters the Offensive Life Cycle

Prevention can stop the Attacker from gaining initial access or persistence. Firewalls, spam filters, personal security products, browser security settings, and technical things, such as the randomization of program memory, are all focused on prevention. Prevention is also exercised via less technical means such as creating a sane network architecture, consistently updating, or training users.

Constraint is the limiting of lateral movement within a network. It counters access persistence and expansion. Constraint can also be thought of as insider threat mitigation, except the insider could be an outside Attacker that has commandeered an employee's access. Requiring most users to use nonadmin accounts is a good example.

Obstruction makes it difficult for the Attacker to get data back out of the network. It is the last hurdle for the Attacker to clear. The current industry buzzwords for this are *data exfiltration prevention* or *data loss prevention*. Imposing bandwidth quotas is a simple example that limits the Attacker's ability to move data out of a network.

Detection is the catchall for finding and recognizing the Attacker during any part of the operational life cycle. Detection can occur from a technical product, such as antivirus, a user noticing an anomaly, auditing various logs, or alerts from intrusion detection systems. There is actually no fixed way to ensure detection, and that is the crux of the problem.

Finally, *response* is the blanket term for actions the Defender takes once they realize they are compromised. There is the immediate response: rooting out and eliminating any traces of the Attacker. But there is also the longer-term response, determining the failures in technology or process that led to the compromise and addressing them.

To date, there is no decent automated way of accomplishing either kind of response, and so an entire industry of so-called incident response companies have sprung up to fill the void.

Though the Defender may fall short at times, these six items—privacy, prevention, constraint, obstruction, detection, and response—form the core of what is necessary to break the offensive operational life cycle. Some are technical; others are not. Some require money, others time, and still others just expertise. The goal is to economize among them such that the defense is effective enough.

Principle of Economy

Like the Attacker, the Defender has a limited amount of time, money, and technical expertise; but unlike the Attacker, the Defender's primary focus may not be security. In fact, contrary to the name, the Defender's focus may have nothing to do with defending.

Most target computer users have a job that takes priority over computer security. Whether it is accounting, human resources, sales, logistics, or engineering, the end user is unlikely to be focused on the computer as a platform that must be defended. It is instead a tool to be used. End users must economize their time, and computer security does not make the list of priorities.

This does not mean that end users will never catch the Attacker. As the saying goes, "even a blind squirrel finds a nut once in a while." It only means that typical end users will not have the experience or even the interest to do so. As long as the Attacker does not interrupt the jobs for which those people are paid, the Attacker is pretty safe.

The computer administrative base is the true Defender. This group is directly responsible for security and, at least for large organizations, probably has a fair amount of expertise and experience in detecting Attackers.

In theory, defending should be easier than attacking, at least that is what Clausewitz[3] posited about land war. Defense has the negative objective to maintain the status quo, whereas the offense must effect some change while being resisted.

In practice, the superior strength of the stasis objective immediately breaks down with information technology. (It also does not hold for long-range artillery, nuclear weapons, and so on, but that is another story.)

This view of conflict assumes a static setup, like a key ridge to take or a river to cross. With computer networks, there are new users, software updates, new software, new devices, and hardware failures that business must keep pace with, sometimes just to stand still. Even the best attempt to keep an environment static cannot prevent some level of dynamism.

Dynamism means the economy of resources will affect the administrator base. The people tasked with security are inevitably tasked with upgrading hardware, making and restoring backups, managing network permissions, answering technical support questions, deploying new software, and more. The Defender must balance all these critical business needs with security.

Economy of resources works against the Defender in subtle ways as well. Security has no immediately visible benefit to the bottom line, the ultimate driver of any business. The cost of a lock is easy to determine, but the benefit is not readily apparent until after a robbery, if ever. And this can be a rather expensive lock. Security done right costs anywhere from thousands to millions of dollars in hardware, software, hiring, and training.

Without overstating it, it is fair to say that the general state of the commercial and industrial base could be categorized as completely negligent not even 15 years ago. Since then, enough locks have been broken (where they existed) that some have taken heed, but even now, many organizations view the risk of compromise as remote enough that they are unwilling to invest much in security, settling for less effective alternatives.

As one executive director of security noted:

> *There are decisions that have to be made. We're trying to remain profitable for our shareholders, and we literally could go broke trying to cover for everything. So, you make risk-based decisions: What're the most important things that are absolutely required by law?*[4]

This budget-focused security attitude is hard for the defensive security community to swallow. These words, uttered by the executive director of Sony Entertainment's security in 2007, were mocked far and wide following a massive compromise in 2014. The stone throwers lined up as Sony gave in to threats and delayed the release of a movie, and as internal e-mails, employee personal information, and unreleased scripts were dumped onto the Internet.

By all accounts Sony's security was egregious, but not necessarily worse than anyone else's. Is the cost of security greater than the potential loss? Clearly not in Sony's case, but what about for everyone else? What is economical to guard against? It is, as quoted above, a "risk-based decision," one that should be based on actual risk and not legal requirements, but a decision nonetheless. It is often not only rational but also correct to limit security when the costs and benefits are meticulously weighed.

All this means that a security-conscious administrator may not be able to command the money and resources necessary to do the job right. Limited resources equals limited security. The principle of economy ensures that the Defender will never devote as much time and attention to security as wanted. The task then becomes finding the right balance, one that enables what the Defender does devote to security to be effective.

The Helpful Defender

This is not a pillar per se, but Defenders cannot help but be helpful. They often may make their own position worse by following "good" business practices.

How exactly? A full accounting is impossible. However, here are a few examples in which Defenders can inadvertently aid Attackers in each part of the offensive operational life cycle.

- **Targeting**—Using a standard naming scheme for e-mail addresses may ease user account tracking, but it also allows Attackers to translate often readily available staff names into an e-mail target list.

- **Access**—Postponing a software update may allow for adequate testing to ensure compatibility and reliability, but it also leaves systems vulnerable for a longer period of time.

- **Persistence**—Upgrading on a fixed schedule may allow the user base to prepare for outages, but it also allows an Attacker to predict and avoid any changes.

- **Expansion**—Centralizing administrative authority to a few user accounts may help lock down insider access, but it also means that a compromise of those accounts will lead to the Attacker gaining full access to the entire network.

- **Exfiltration**—Allowing people to access the web may improve morale or research productivity, but it also leaves open a potential Attacker communication path.

Each previous action is taken for good reason, but all these actions turn the Defender into an unwitting helper. The three first principles—the necessity of access, the inherent humanity, and the limitations of economy—all but force the Defender into this awkward helpful position.

Summary

The first principles of humanity, access, and economy all work against the Defender. Together they guarantee that there is no perfect technical solution to security that can be implemented by people with limited resources. However, it is not hopeless, as the Attacker is subject to the same principles. The differing application of these principles by each side gives each advantages over the other. In the next chapter, we'll explore what some of the more important advantages are.

CHAPTER 4

Asymmetries

And he had a helmet of brass upon his head, and he was armed with a coat of mail...greaves of brass upon his legs, and a target of brass between his shoulders... [And David] took thence a stone, and slang it, and smote the Philistine in his forehead...and he fell upon his face to the earth.

—1 Samuel 17

Some 3,000 years ago, Goliath took the field of battle securely armed and prepared for hand-to-hand combat. He then fell victim to perhaps the world's most famous remote attacker. David exploited an advantage in striking distance to strike one of Goliath's few exposed vulnerabilities. And had he missed, David would have surely launched the other four stones he held before Goliath could have closed the distance to engage. As Malcolm Gladwell noted in his 2013 book *David and Goliath: Underdogs, Misfits, and the Art of Battling Giants* (Little, Brown and Company), it was not a fair fight. Goliath was at a *disadvantage* because he did not understand the asymmetry of the encounter.

To understand the success of computer attacks and the failure of computer security, you must move beyond thinking in terms of a specific event or security failure and understand the properties of the space. To read the news, you would think that every time a company divulges its customers' personal data, exposes sensitive internal e-mails, or loses the design to yet another advanced weapons system, that the compromise was inevitable. *This attitude is lazy.*

Warring technologies have historically leapfrogged each other: from cavalry over foot soldiers, to tanks over cavalry, to A-10s over tanks, which may someday be rendered ineffective by rail guns. Judging from the 600+ known data breaches in 2013 alone,[1] Attackers in CNE have an empirical advantage, but is that guaranteed to last? Why or why not? Which imbalances are foregone conclusions and which are worth fighting? Load up your slingshot and let's take a look.

False Asymmetries

The oft-repeated refrain—excuse, actually—of the security community is along the lines of "The Attacker has to be right only once. The Defender has to be right all the time." That is true, but the same is equally true for Fort Knox. After all, an Attacker needs to get through security only once to steal a gold bar from the U.S. supply. How is cyberspace different?

The oft-repeated answer is that cyberspace is inherently asymmetric, unlike the physical world. This is almost always followed by pointing out two things: cost and attribution. Neither is a true asymmetry.[2]

Cost

Attacking is supposedly cheap, whereas defending is expensive. The implication is that Attackers can just trip over their keyboard and produce a magic exploit that can defeat every organization's security. Perhaps in the early days of the Internet, this was not far from the truth, but today this is nonsense.

Attacking is cheap only in the way that driving a car a few miles is cheap. If you consider only the cost of the gasoline to the owner, driving costs just a few dollars. But add in the cost of manufacturing the car, and it jumps to tens of thousands. Yet even this is not the true cost. Billions of dollars have been invested over decades to build the mining operations, manufacturing plants, oil refineries, roads, gas stations, and more that all precipitate hopping in your car to go pick up milk.

Offensive operations are cheaper than building an entire automotive infrastructure, but the analogy is valid. Breaking into a particular network may be cheap after the tools and infrastructure are in place. Top off the gas and off you go. However, some aspects do not last much longer than that gallon of milk. Building and maintaining the infrastructure for a program of sustained operations requires targeting, research, hardware engineering, software development, analysis, and training. This is not cheap, nor is it a game of luck.

Attackers do not stumble into being "right once." They put in the time and effort to build an infrastructure and then work through Thomas Edison's alleged "10,000 ways that won't work." Cost is simply not as asymmetric as many contend.

Still, various sources put combined Defender spending on IT-related security at 50 to 70 billion dollars a year, a figure that surpasses what each country in the world, excluding the top 5, spends on their armed forces. And yet the defense still fails, rather spectacularly. This is because individual defense expenditures do not improve the overall security of the space. One company's improvements do not benefit others. Another company's hard-learned lessons do not permeate.

The supposed asymmetry of cost is actually just lack of defensive coordination.

Attribution

Attribution is typically mentioned as the next asymmetry. Perfect attribution is indeed difficult. The architecture of the Internet makes it such.

As data moves across the Internet, it is forwarded through proxies and subjected to network address translation (NAT). At a high level, NAT works as shown in Figure 4.1.

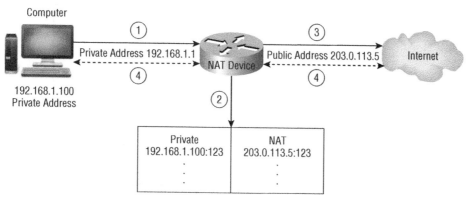

1. A computer with private address 192.168.1.100 attempts to contact the website www.example.com. The request is sent to the NAT device.

2. The source address and network port of the request is recorded in a table.

3. The NAT device initiates its own request to www.example.com and records its own source address and network port.

4. The session is established. Data is sent and received through the NAT device using the table to rewrite addresses as appropriate.

Figure 4.1: Network address translation

You can identify the NAT device from the outside, but tracing further inwards requires two things:

▪ The NAT device needs to store logs of the transaction.

▪ The cooperation of whomever owns the NAT device.

There are various technical methods of trying to distinguish different computers behind a NAT device based on the differences between operating systems, web browser configurations, timing, and so forth. While these methods allow someone to identify a unique computer, without logs of the transaction, it still does not reveal the source address of the connection.

The real world problem is even harder. NAT devices are often layered as shown in Figure 4.2.

For example, right now my computer is behind two layers of indirection: one for my home network and one for the ISP. It isn't until the third hop, after the source address has been rewritten twice, that a data packet leaving my computer reaches the public Internet. To attribute that packet to my home network, someone must first get the cooperation of the ISP. Then, to attribute it to this computer, someone would need *my* cooperation.

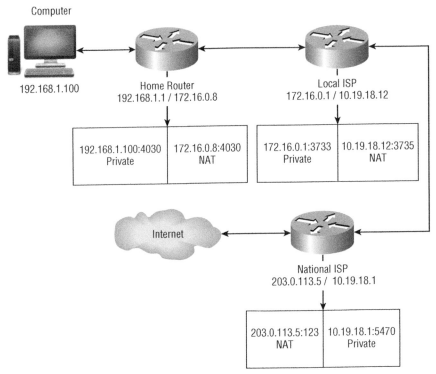

Figure 4.2: Layered network address translation

And therein lies the problem. Tracing a connection requires the cooperation of every entity from the public-facing IP address inward. This may be forthcoming in a criminal investigation if it is within a single country. (There's no question Verizon would give up my records if served a warrant from the FBI.)

Cooperation might be possible between allied countries. But it all breaks down as soon you start crossing international boundaries between rival countries. Attribution then requires cooperation from state-controlled (or influenced) communications companies without any legal basis to compel them. (If anything, there may be legal issues that prevent them from cooperating.) The trail will stop there.

And this is just the basic Internet addressing system. It ignores the reality that the Attacker will take active steps to misdirect the Defender. These steps include forwarding connections through multiple countries, using fake and/ or real companies, launching from or routing through cloud service providers such as Amazon Web Services, or leveraging innocent but compromised third-party networks. These and other techniques provide further protection against attribution.

Of course, even with careful offensive planning, some attributive characters can be determined over time, such as country of origin. More specific details may be found with mistakes or lapses in operational security. But these are the exception, and they often require months to piece together. It remains difficult to attribute the source of an attack in real time.

So, yes, attribution is more difficult than in the physical world. But *so what*?

Suppose attribution were not an issue. There is nothing so permanent about technology that ordains the current state of anonymity. Recently, Verizon and AT&T were revealed to be adding "Unique Identifier Headers" to their customers' browsing to de-anonymize and track it. They backed away when it became public, but you can easily imagine a larger shift occurring that slides all traffic away from anonymity. Many countries and advertising companies are attempting to do just that.

What does full attribution change? In the physical world, the North Koreans continued to deny sinking a South Korean naval vessel even after incontrovertible proof was presented. The Russian government maintained that it had no troops in Crimea despite the presence of Russian tanks, Russian-speaking uniformed soldiers with Russian weapons, and at least one soldier on film answering, "Yes" to the question, "Are you a Russian solider?" And that is in a world with established international norms and laws of war. The virtual world doesn't have the benefit of having such precedents to ignore.

Nation-states maintain their innocence with an ever-weakening shield of plausible deniability as the mountains of evidence pile up against them. Report after report gives ever more detail about so-called "threat actors." Still the attacks continue.

Perhaps attribution could cut into purely criminal activities. It might give some pause for CNA. But do not expect blame to slow down espionage. A true asymmetry provides one side an advantage of sorts. The difficulty of attribution provides no such benefit to espionage as evidenced by the fact that when caught, behavior does not change. Therefore, it is a false asymmetry.

Advantage Attacker

A true asymmetry provides a strategic advantage to one side. It is difficult to counter, but if successfully countered, it causes behavioral changes to the formerly advantaged side. Cost is not nearly as unbalanced as first perceived. Attribution, even if solved, it not going to make much impact on espionage. But just because these two are fakes does not preclude actual imbalances.

Here are some true asymmetries that are to the Attacker's advantage.

Motivation

Consider two lottery games. The first game, call it Fifty Plus, gives a 50 percent chance of winning. The cost of the ticket may be substantial, but odds are good you will recoup more than you invest. In the worst case, you lose the cost of the ticket. Fifty Plus is all upside.

The second game, call this one Zero Minus, gives a 0 percent chance of winning. Losing the cost of the ticket is the best possible outcome. The worst outcome is you lose the investment *and* some additional unknown amount of money, ranging from nothing to all your income. This loss happens all at once, over several years, or maybe never. Zero Minus is all downside.

Which game would you be excited to play? A nation-state is playing the first game. Sure there are costs, but there is a huge payoff potential and little risk. The gains are immediate and tangible.

The Defender is playing the second game. There is nothing to gain, only something to lose. And the nature of the loss is often intangible, ranging from nothing to catastrophic.

The difference between the two risk reward trade-offs creates an imbalance in motivation. With attacking, the Attacker accomplishes something tangible: gaining access, retrieving some piece of data, or outsmarting some person or system. With defending, if the Defender is successful, nothing happens. That's hardly inspirational.

Of course, there is also a third game, call it the Crime Pays version. This version is variable risk and high reward. There's a good chance of success, but there is also a chance of getting arrested.

The stakes in Crime Pays vary widely. The probability of arrest depends on the criminal's home country. Some countries seem to tolerate, if not encourage, electronic theft. There is some risk, such as when Roman Valerevich Seleznev, a.k.a. "Track2," an alleged trafficker in stolen financial information, was arrested in Guam.[3] But that risk is small. You can safely bet Track2, a son of a Russian Parliament member, would have been protected from arrest had he stayed in Russia.

Others countries, like the United States with its FBI, do their best to track down what they can. The odds of arrest are much higher. Between the two extremes are countries like Romania, where criminal behavior is widespread, but occasionally someone gets taken down.

The potential personal risk in this game has an interesting selection effect: the unmotivated stay out. Only the highly motivated are willing to take the risk. This means that criminals, if anything, are likely to be the most motivated party out there. They are motivated both by success and fear of failure.

The Defender is also motivated by fear of failure, but people are simply not as viscerally inspired to protect some indeterminate company loss as they are to protect their own skin.

The stakes involved in the three versions are not the only issue. The Defender suffers from a further demotivator: monotony. Much of defending is repetitive.

Checking logs, updating software, or applying patches are all tasks that need to be done over and over. Sure there is designing and expanding the network, integrating new systems, or finding and purging an intruder, but this only means that occasionally the Defender has the same level of motivation as the Attacker.

Of course, higher motivation for the Attacker in itself does not guarantee success: I am not going to beat Michael Jordan in a game of one-on-one no matter how much more motivated I may be. But motivation drives investment, recruitment, creativity, attention to detail, and a host of other things that make a substantial difference to which side prevails.

Initiative

Initiative is having the ability to make threats or take actions that require your opponent to react. It is different than motivation. *Motivation* describes mental state, whereas *initiative* measures ability.

The Attacker has the initiative. An exploit is released and a patch follows. An attack methodology becomes known, and an operating system mitigation is developed. A Trojan is found and a signature is created. By and large, the Attacker acts and the Defender reacts.

Having the initiative means that the Attacker can stay one step ahead. The Conficker worm provides an example. The Conficker worm was a piece of Microsoft Windows malware that infected millions of computers across industry and government starting at the end of 2008. The worm included an update mechanism that would reach out to potential Internet rendezvous points for new code. Each day the worm generated and contacted a list of 250 pseudorandom domain names for new updates.

The security community responded quickly. Within approximately 3 months, it had fully reverse engineered the name-generation algorithm and locked down all potential contact addresses. It was a momentous, timely, and effective effort.

But think about how much time that actually is: 3 months. Three months from *discovery*. The Attacker had 3 entire months to update Conficker and adapt while the Defender reacted. And update it they did, releasing B, C, D, and E variants at a rate of about one per month, each improving on the last.

How long had the exploit been used before that? Who knows? The flaw existed in Windows 2000 SP4 for at least 5 *years* before public discovery. There is simply no way to know if or how long one Attacker managed to keep it quiet before another made it into a worm.

Scenarios like this are fairly common. According to the 2012 Symantec study "Before We Knew It: An Empirical Study of Zero-Day Attacks in the Real World," a previously unknown exploit (a Zero-Day) is used for between 19 days and 30 months, with an average of 10 months and a median of 8.[4] Immunity Security published a report stating that the average was over 1 year. Either way, that means the Attacker can expect well over one-half year of initiative per exploit. That is quite an advantage.

The Defender can attempt to take the initiative, and it's not like the security community is sitting idly by. In 2011, Microsoft, in conjunction with the U.S. Marshals, FireEye security company, the University of Washington, and partners in the Netherlands and China successfully launched a legal and technical counterattack that decapitated the Rustock botnet in one fell swoop.

This act of striking initiative undoubtedly took the botnet's masters by surprise. So the Defender can take initiative. It is just more difficult because it requires greater resources and coordination. The Attacker, however, does not require coordination. Therefore, until such time as this coordination is no longer required, the Attacker will maintain an asymmetric advantage in initiative.

Focus

The Attacker has a single mission and point of focus. Although that focus may be split among building capabilities and different operations, their focus is always on gaining, maintaining, and exploiting access.

Attackers also have positive feedback that reinforces focus. Attackers know when they gain access, when they fail, and when they lose access. This feedback enables them to adjust and try again, all while maintaining focus on the objective. Feedback keeps people focused and glued to the task—just ask the gambling and gaming industries.

Defenders, however, have their focus split between securing the network and running it. Similarly, technology companies have their focus split between developing secure versus timely and functional products.

Further, Defenders lack positive feedback. They know for certain only when they fail. Although you may detect one attack, there is no way to prove that you detected all attacks, that a successful intrusion did not occur. You cannot prove a negative. The feedback that the proverbial barn door is open comes only when Defenders notice the horse (that is, their data) galloping across the field. This difference in feedback and reinforcement serves only to exacerbate the existing difference in focus.

Therefore, due to singularity of purpose and feedback, Attackers have an asymmetric advantage in focus.

Effect of Failure

In classical war theory, when close combat dominated war, defense was considered the stronger form of warfare. It is easier to hold a prepared position than to advance into one. This conclusion contains a key assumption: fending off an attack has an impact on the Attacker. Each unsuccessful attack carries some risk and leads to fatigue, equipment damage, casualties, or other spent resources.

This assumption is invalid for computer operations. Preventing an attack may have no effect whatsoever on the Attacker.

The Defender may prevent an intrusion without ever detecting that an attack was attempted. Perhaps the attack was blocked outright by the firewall. Perhaps the web application was secure enough to withstand SQL injection attacks. Perhaps the e-mail-luring e-mail was blocked by the spam filter. The failed attack may not even be logged. When Defenders do not know they were attacked, the only impact on the Attacker is loss of time.

The Defender may catch and stop the attack early in the process. Perhaps that malicious e-mail attachment is caught by antivirus as soon as it is opened. In this case, only the initial access tool is lost, or worst case the outermost layer of the attack infrastructure. The exploit used to gain execution and the core infrastructure likely remain completely operational, as do the more advanced tools never installed that would have followed. Again, the only real loss to the Attacker is time.

This lack of impact on the Attacker is the theory behind honeypots. A *honeypot* is a computer network designed to entice Attackers in, to trick them into exposing a larger cadre of tools and methods in the hopes of inflicting a cost. Honeypots can be effective, but they have historically been expensive. Creating an entirely new network that is convincing enough to appear real is no small feat.

Generally though, an Attacker loses little in trying, failing, and waking up the next day to try again. There is no real impact on resources. Beyond that, the risk of legal or other consequences is essentially nonexistent. (Notwithstanding, the United States recently filed criminal charges against five members of the PLA. However, there is no expectation that this will immediately impact Chinese espionage; rather it is simply the first step in a broader program of enforcing consequences.)

By contrast, the effect of failing to prevent an attack can be devastating to the Defender. Trade secrets may be lost, customer confidence destroyed, money stolen, or business negotiating positions weakened, among other outcomes.

Unfortunately, even if the Defender successfully prevents an intrusion, they may be weakened. Attackers learn from their failures and adjust. Was the e-mail opened? What led to being stopped? Where are the public points of presence? Was the exploit stopped by a firewall? Which brand? How long did it take the Defender to react? Attackers may glean all this and more from an unsuccessful operation and put it to use on the next attempt.

The Defender has no such knowledge to gain from a single unsuccessful attack. Certainly you may learn how the Attacker attempted (or successfully gained) access the last time, but this tells you little about the next go-around. It requires a substantial amount of data across many attacks to even begin to make any kind of prediction about future methods.

The Attacker has little to lose and much to gain even in failure. The Defender has little to gain and much to lose. The effect of failure is asymmetric.

Knowledge of Technology

A well-funded Attacker knows more about common technology than the typical Defender. This is because the Attacker has a much broader base of experience having "worked on" more disparate networks than the typical system administrator. As you move from one network to the next, the commonalities become second nature. Whether it is router configurations, Windows Active Directory trees, LDAP configurations, types of mail servers, file servers, and such, there are but a limited number of typical setups, and the Attacker has seen them all.

This knowledge imbalance is even more certain for knowledge of how to break systems. Offense is the Attacker's full-time job. Some administrators may read about offense. Others may explore it as a hobby. But how many will spend most of their waking hours living and breathing offensive computer security like the Attacker? Few, and those few will be the exception.

Perhaps surprisingly, the Attacker is also more likely to understand defensive technologies, including how to effectively deploy them. Why? Defensive technology is part of both the Attacker's and the Defender's job, but there is a difference in motivation. The Defender must learn defensive methods and technologies to stay current and to maintain compliance. The Attacker must learn them to stay in business. You could, of course, argue the same thing for the Defender, but the urgency just is not there.

There is, however, one critical exception in the asymmetry of technical knowledge: if the Defender employs proprietary or rare technology. If no one else runs a particular package, then clearly the Attacker will know little about it at the onset. Here the Defender has an advantage, at least while their institutional knowledge of the system remains. This small plus, however, is often offset by the generally weaker security found in uncommon applications or by the additional complexity created by using nonstandard technology.

Knowledge of technology is clearly not an inherent asymmetry. A well-resourced Defender is capable of knowing just as much as the Attacker. In some sense though, it is just a reflection of motivation. At present, the Attacker is more motivated and as a consequence almost certainly more knowledgeable.

Analysis of Opponent

It is relatively easy for the Attacker to acquire and analyze defensive software and devices. For approximately $500, you can buy the top 10 personal security products that make up the majority of endpoint installations. For $500 K you can get the commercial versions and a consequential selection of defensive hardware. For $5 M—a lot for a small company but hardly a stretch for a large company or government—you can purchase practically every piece of software and a substantial portion of the hardware that is commercially available.

Of course, some things are not (easily) commercially available, such as high-end telecommunications gear, SCADA systems common in manufacturing, or other proprietary systems. Yet on balance, the bulk of any security is most likely made up of off-the-shelf components. So in general, Attackers can acquire, analyze, and test against these solutions before deploying their attack tools.

Also, the Defender's high-level technology choices tend to be quite stable, which can make analysis even easier. Switching between Cisco and Huawei hardware across an organization or between McAfee and Symantec software is a substantial undertaking. It will not be fast nor frequent. Attackers have basically as much time as they need for analyzing this high-level technology, limited only by how long a particular version of it will remain deployed.

The same ease of acquisition is not available to the Defender. Offensive tools are not for sale, at least not on open commercial markets. Yes, there are underground markets, where a single exploit purportedly can sell for $100,000 or more,[5] but not all Defenders can pay this price, and few attack tools are generally available even if they could. The underground industry is smart enough to understand that if tools are available, security companies will just buy up the stock and protect against them. This would not be good for the purveyors' reputations or their business models.

In practical terms, offensive tools, at least the ones that are going to be used against you, cannot be purchased. They must be captured. This leads to a chicken-and-egg type problem: you must detect and capture a tool for analysis, but you must analyze the tool to detect and capture it. This circle often leaves the defensive industry stuck detecting the previous generation of tools.

Of course, it's not quite that cut and dry and hopeless. Defenders catch unknown tools all the time by looking for reused components and methodologies or variations of the two. This kind of analysis is done by pattern recognition and prediction. It works to an extent and is constantly improving, but it does not undo the fundamental imbalance. Defenders must guess and predict. Attackers simply purchase and know. Attackers have a fundamental advantage in analyzing their opponent.

Tailored Software

Consider the software at the so-called pointy end: software used to gain and maintain access and exfiltrate data for the offense, and software used to prevent this for the defense.

Attacker development is tailored to the task at hand. Whether it's a remote access tool, collector, or method of persisting, the Attacker controls the process from start to finish. There is only one set of users, one set of requirements, and one set of well-defined use cases. For anyone familiar with the process of software development, these limitations confer a huge advantage in speed.

The entire development life cycle can be compressed. Without outside customers, polish can be traded for functionality and reliability. Tools can be developed to meet the minimal requirements and then later expanded without worrying about how to attract customers. Testing can be done just-in-time when a new setup is encountered instead of having to test all potential situations up front. Training can be done across the entire user base. User feedback can be queried directly.

The Attacker's support tail is more flexible. Tools that outlive their usefulness can be abandoned entirely. Think about when a company discontinues a product line with an avid user base. Windows XP was released in 2001 and supported for 13 years. During 7 of those years, there was a replacement available (Windows Vista), and during 5 of those there was a decent replacement available (Windows 7). Cisco supports their hardware products for 5 years after they stop selling them entirely.

Commercial companies have to issue warnings of deprecation, develop upgrade paths, and provide long-term support. Attackers may do all this, or they may just throw the whole thing in the trash. There is no concern for damaging an external reputation. There is no need to convince users to spend more money for an upgrade. Attackers can make the most efficient decisions necessary without regard for losing market share.

Of course, just because Attackers can be efficient does not mean they will be. All the previously mentioned advantages presuppose nimble Attackers with decisive management and whose development and operational elements can effectively communicate. This ideal is hard to meet in organizations of any consequence. But the only thing limiting the Attackers' speed of development for pointy-end software is their resources and themselves.

This is in contrast to defensive tools. Defenders must wait for the commercial market to develop tools, a process that is typically a 1–2 year life cycle. Significant updates, in the best case, are quarterly. Nor are these out-of-the-box tools customized for Defenders. How could they be? Most tools need to appeal to a broad market to be profitable. So Defenders must take extra steps to adapt defensive tools to their particular scenario after delivery.

In short, Attackers have an advantage in creating and deploying pointy-end software. The development cycle can be condensed and it is under their own control. However, this advantage is not inherent. The defensive security market is actively researching and developing defensive architectures that can be quickly tailored to specific environments under the buzzword *adaptive defense*. Results so far have been muted, but it is in the early stages. If and when a true adaptive defense is achieved, the Attackers' advantage will dissipate.

Rate of Change

The fast pace of technological change works to the Attackers' advantage. The Attackers' superior focus, motivation, and initiative gives them, almost by definition, the ability to act faster, to adapt, and to exploit. But that advantage has been covered in previous sections, so why call out rate of change separately? The rapidity of change yields another asymmetry: a shifting security foundation.

In the physical world, security is additive. If there is a locked safe, putting it in a locked room and then posting a guard at the entrance enhances the security of the safe. Each new layer builds upon the previous foundation and makes the whole system more effective.

This intuitive understanding of security does not translate to the virtual world. The massive increase in computing power and the corresponding increase in the system and software complexity guarantees there is simply no solid foundation to build upon. The pace of change prevents it.

In 2014, the world was introduced to Heartbleed. This bug affected OpenSSL, a software program used across the world to establish secure connections between web browsers and websites. (You are using SSL or the Secure Sockets Layer when you see the secure lock icon or the green highlighting in your browser. OpenSSL is a popular implementation of this protocol.) The bug allowed Attackers to read information out of a server's memory, information like passwords and credit card numbers.

The bug was introduced in March 2012, and subsequently discovered and patched in April 2014. Putting aside the technical details of how it worked, consider only the chain of events. A software program, whose sole purpose is establishing trust, is made more vulnerable by an update, and it takes more than 2 years before anyone notices. Security is clearly not additive.

This simple fact is what makes the comparison of virtual security to the physical security of somewhere like Fort Knox invalid. When Fort Knox's defenses are updated, they are added to a well-established foundation. They do not weaken previously deployed defenses. However, when software is updated, especially if new features are added, history has shown there's a decent chance new vulnerabilities will be introduced.

The rate of change and the resultant shaky foundation it creates offers a renewing stream of vulnerabilities that is to the Attacker's advantage. The pace could theoretically work to the Defender's advantage if the Attacker fell behind. But so far this has not been an issue, and it is unlikely to become one while the Attacker maintains an advantage in motivation and focus.

Advantage Defender

The Attacker has many natural advantages over Defenders, but they do not hold all the cards. There are a few areas in which Defenders have their own favorable asymmetries.

Network Awareness

The network is the Defender's home court. User log-ons, network traffic, application use, and other information can all be logged, monitored, and analyzed. The Defender has the ability to have complete network awareness, and with that ability, the Defender is capable of ferreting out the Attacker.

Of course, exercising this ability requires time, money, expertise, and the adeptness to intelligently avoid information overload. There is a wide gap between the potential of total awareness and the reality of it that is rarely closed. For example, many companies do not even have a basic high-level drawing of their own network layout when asked for it by assessment teams. If you do not understand how your network is put together, there is no hope of finding an intrusion. Nonetheless, it is within the sole power of the Defender to close this gap, and at least in theory, it is always possible to detect the Attacker.

The Attacker lacks this level of capability. They simply cannot acquire the same level of detail with the same level of effort. Everything is more difficult. The Defender can read the manufacturer and model number of a router off the label, while the Attacker has to figure this out from surveys and profiling tools. The Defender can collect and search hard drives full of monitoring information, whereas the Attacker has no practical method of getting this information.

Now in some instances, the Attacker may actually understand the network better than administrators. As the Attacker enumerates and navigates the network, their information is dynamically refreshed. Meanwhile, the Defenders' information may grow stale. But this is merely an advantage of circumstance and effort in spite of the asymmetry, not because of it.

The Defender has full access to every switch, every router, every firewall configuration, and every computer. If leveraged with the right tools and expertise, this level of access and awareness can be a dominant advantage.

Network Posture

Defenders can change the constraints of the network at any time and in any manner. It is not just their home court. They can make and remake the court and its rules at will.

Posture changes can range from the simple, such as changing a password, to the complex, such as segmenting portions of the network. New network layouts, security technologies, auditing, or the tightening of technical and nontechnical policies and controls can all be introduced with impunity. The Attacker cannot prevent the Defender from doing anything.

By contrast, the Attacker must expend significant time and effort to keep from being blinded by changes in network posture. The introduction of a firewall rule, the decommissioning of a switch, or the updating of a single computer can set back Attackers if they are not careful.

This disparity of control opens a theoretical way of keeping the Attacker off balance. A moving target is harder to hit. The concept of keeping things in motion has been applied with some success on a microscale through antiexploitation technologies such as address space layout randomization (ASLR). At a high level, ASLR changes how programs are loaded, making certain classes of vulnerabilities much harder to exploit without affecting the program itself.

Creating a moving target is a powerful idea. To date, however, there is little that leverages an analogous concept across a network. The challenge, of course, is how to effectively randomize an entire network in such a way that it still functions as expected for the user base but confuses the Attacker. Is this possible? It's an open question. Either way, more could be done to effectively leverage the asymmetric advantage of control of network posture.

Advantage Indeterminate

It's 6:00 p.m., and the local high school football game is about to start on a field that runs east-west. It's clear that one team is going to have the sun in its eyes the entire first half, and by the time it switches sides, the sun will have set and it will not be an issue for their opponents.

Some asymmetries are like that. One side will have an advantage, but until the coin is tossed, it's impossible to know which. These asymmetries are worth mentioning, if only to be aware of how factors outside one's control set the stage.

Time

Time constraints are rarely symmetric. For the Attacker, time is required to understand the target and hide, expand, and complete the objective. Every stage of the operation requires time. The Attacker also needs times to develop the technology and methodologies necessary to execute an operation.

The urgency of the operation varies considerably with the operational objective. If the objective is strategic in nature, such as stealing intellectual property, perhaps the Attacker has months or even years to infiltrate. They can just keep pounding away like waves against a sea wall until eventually a breakthrough is found. This is allegedly how China is operating within many U.S. industrial and technology sectors: slowly and patiently.

If the operation is tactical in nature, time may be more constrained. Interdicting a shipment of weapons or gaining insight into a country's political system can have rather strict deadlines.

With more time, Attackers can develop better capabilities and improve their access in a network, or their existing abilities can atrophy and they can become more exposed. Time can help and it can hurt.

By contrast, Defenders need time to maintain the network and update, upgrade, and expand it. They need time to build and maintain expertise, train new employees, and create and implement secure processes. Defenders also needs time to find, analyze, and counter Attackers.

With more time, Defenders can strengthen their perimeter and internal controls or grow more complacent. They can seek out existing infiltrations, or remain blissfully unaware as the Attacker burrows ever deeper.

Which side has the advantage? There are simply too many variables to make a blanket assertion. What is certain is that time is not under the full control of either party. The Attacker dictates the Defender's time line and vice versa, while the technology drives both. It is an asymmetric advantage that is up for grabs.

Efficiency

Efficiency is a measure of how well an organization performs against some criteria within the given time constraints.

For an efficient Attacker, interim criteria may include the total number of simultaneous targets, the depth of penetration, the number of times detected, the speed of new technology development and deployment, or any number of other metrics. The ultimate criteria is the value of whatever information is gathered measured against the cost of gaining it, as shown in Figure 4.3.

Cost of Acquiring Information

Value of Information Acquired

Figure 4.3: Attacker efficiency criteria

Compromising 500 pizza delivery places sounds impressive but is unlikely to have the same value as the intellectual property of a major chemical manufacturer.

For the Defender, interim criteria may include the speed and efficacy of patching or the lag time between compromise and detection. The ultimate criteria is the value of whatever information is secured measured against the cost of securing it, as shown in Figure 4.4.

Figure 4.4: Defender efficiency criteria

Efficiency varies widely. Attackers may range from loose-knit criminal organizations to professional intelligence organizations, though which is more efficient is not a given. Larger organizations have the capability to be more efficient through scale (think Wal-Mart) but they can get bogged down under the weight of their own processes (think your cable company). Defenders can vary just the same.

It is impossible to generalize which side has the advantage. Are most Attackers more efficient than most Defenders? Yes, if you count the number of attacking organizations versus the number of organizations hacked. But what if you count the number of people that produce offensive technology versus the number that produces defensive technology? Then the answer is not so clear. Maybe the Attackers are not nearly as efficient as presumed.

While generalizing is impossible, one side will most certainly be more efficient for a given Attacker/Defender matchup. Therefore, efficiency is an indeterminate asymmetry. An organization must improve its efficiency in the hope that it gives itself an advantage over its opponent.

Summary

People commonly cite cost and attribution as the great asymmetries in cyber space, but these are strategically irrelevant. Cost is not as cheap as it seems, and attribution is unlikely to change behavior. The true asymmetries are in motivation, initiative, focus, and other areas broader than the specifics of the technology. Recognizing which asymmetries are intrinsic versus those that just reflect current circumstances is the essential first step in minimizing, maximizing, or reversing these advantages outright.

In the next chapter, we'll examine the things that impede the Attacker in spite of their many asymmetric advantages.

Attacker Frictions

Ain't nothin' gonna break my stride.

Nobody's gonna slow me down, oh-no

I got to keep on moving

—Matthew Wilder, American musician, composer, and record producer

Long ago the Prussian general Carl von Clausewitz defined the frictions of war as the "only concept that more or less corresponds to the factors that distinguish real war from war on paper." *Frictions* are the unseen forces that act against movement and progress. The textbook example is an unpredicted patch of mud that bogs down the advance of a tank.

Although there's no mud involved, Computer Network Exploitation shares a few characteristics with war. There are opposing sides that plan and execute objectives. There are differing levels of resources, expertise, and experience. The software, hardware, and network systems involved are dynamic and so complex as to contain elements of unpredictability. These similarities make the model of the frictions of war useful for understanding CNE.

By definition, frictions are not predictable. A predictable friction would simply be an obstacle: something that careful planning can avoid. A firewall is not a friction. Its effects are entirely foreseeable and testable. A change in the set of firewall rules, however, is, especially if there is no advanced warning.

Frictions cannot be avoided, but that does not mean you must face them in ignorance. Certain classes of frictions occur frequently enough that they are worth contemplating when formulating an offensive strategy.

Mistakes

All people make mistakes. That much is obvious. Yet too often the media portrays Attackers as unerring machines. Attackers are no different than everyone else. If not for a mistake in the frequency of propagation, the famed Morris worm would have likely remained an intellectual exercise instead of taking down the better part of the Internet in 1988.

Mistakes can be made in all aspects of the operational life cycle. Attackers may target the wrong set of networks. They may miss vulnerable services and focus on harder aspects for initial access. They may pull too much data and alert the administrators, execute the wrong commands, mistype addresses, and so on.

Mistakes are what get Attackers caught. The hacker Hector Xavier Monsegur, better known as Sabu, a cofounder of the hacking group LulzSec, managed to forget to anonymize his connection to a chat room.[1] The FBI came knocking on his door shortly thereafter.

The North Koreans, allegedly, repeated a similar error while hacking Sony Entertainment in 2014.[2] The authors of the Flame malware that permeated the Middle East left behind various clues on command and control servers, despite their attempts to wipe them clean.[3] No Attacker, no matter how skilled, is immune.

Many mistakes can be eliminated through technology, training, experience, establishment of and adherence to processes, two-man verification, or strong consequences. Some can be mitigated by building intentional limitations or "Are you sure you want to do this?" type safeguards directly into attack tools. Other mistakes can be reduced by ensuring appropriate levels of redundancy.

In essence, the Attacker can try any combination of systems and methods that people have devised over thousands of years to try and eliminate mistakes, yet some will still occur. And their consequences will not always be easy to predict. Despite more than $300 million and countless brilliant people, NASA still managed to crash the Mars Climate Orbiter. Why? Because one software system measured thrust in pound-seconds, an English measure of impulse, while another expected it in newton-seconds, the metric equivalent. This was apparently missed in review, simulations, and whatever testing was performed.

No matter the effort expended, mistakes will remain a source of friction.

Complexity

Attackers begin an operation with an information deficit. The network layout, software versions, defensive posture, security policies, user behavioral patterns, and so forth are all unknown, or at best unverified. Even after initial access is obtained and Attackers start performing reconnaissance from inside the network, it takes time to clear the fog. During this critical period of information gathering, anything that is complex, nonstandard, or simply different from the Attackers' experience may slow them down or cause them to expose themselves. The complexity that makes a network harder to manage, also makes it harder to exploit.

A more complex organization may require a wider diversity of tools for success. It certainly requires a broader set of knowledge. For example, Attackers may have a complete tool set and standard operating procedures for a network composed uniformly of, say, Cisco routers and Microsoft Windows technologies (Windows, SQL Server, Exchange Email, IIS, and so on). This setup is encountered often enough that compromising it becomes rote. Now take the same network layout and add in Apple computers, Linux Servers, Solaris with Oracle databases, perhaps a touch of Huawei and Juniper routers, toss in a stack of proprietary internal applications, and now the path forward is far from clear. Each step through the network requires a different set of tools and skills.

To be clear, it is not that a complex or nonstandard setup is more secure. It is generally the opposite. Complex setups eschew thorough review, and custom applications are notoriously poorly written. (In my experience, a skilled security tester and reverse engineer takes less than a week to find flaws in a proprietary application.)

It is simply that complexity may make operational elements such as expansion, analysis, and exfiltration more expensive. Complexity requires more time, knowledge, and development to survey, understand, and circumvent. Because the level of complexity is difficult to predict and can severely impact the efficiency of an operation, it is a friction.

Flawed Attack Tools

All software of any consequence has flaws. There have been books written, methods and tools developed and refined, and even entire computer languages invented in an attempt to combat this truism. Even a perfect programmer, a truly mythical being, is still subject to a flawed foundation. There have been countless vulnerabilities in Windows, Linux, and the Java Virtual Machine, all foundational technologies upon which other programs are built. Developing perfect software is always a worthy goal, but it is an unattainable goal.

Attack tools are not exempt. If anything, attack tools are more likely to have flaws. The Attacker has imperfect information about the deployed environment, wide variability between environments, and most importantly, an inability to control that environment. You cannot force the target to delay an update, or perhaps install one, just because the current system is incompatible with your rootkit.

Also, attack tools often intentionally violate operating system expectations, compatibility, and other constraints leading to unpredictability and instability. And this is the best case, when nothing is attempting to frustrate their actions. Operating systems and security software introduce intentional roadblocks and choke points to identify and neutralize malicious software. Overcoming these requires creating attacks against the system itself, something often extremely version specific. As Microsoft noted in a blog post about the Alureon rootkit:

> *Malware writers use unsupported and potentially destabilizing methods for compromising machines because they want to keep their malware hidden from anti-malware software.*[4]

Most exploits (software that takes advantage of a vulnerability) are unreliable by nature. Think of it from a high level: an exploit writer must reliably reproduce a flaw that even the producers of the technology, the people who presumably understand the system best, could not find. And that's just to get started. Variations in processing speed, amount of memory, system load, and network latency can affect the reliability of an exploit even with a fixed operating system and software install.

In theory, this reliability could be addressed through testing and refinement, especially if the testing is automated. But the lack of control over the environment, variability of systems, and sensitivity to slight differences combine to make attack tool testing onerous. Now add in that some tools require proving a negative (show that a stealth tool cannot be detected or that a failed exploit will not crash a system), and testing descends to occupy one of Dante's nine circles.

Flaws are simply unavoidable. So the question becomes how do they manifest and affect an operation?

Flaws exhibit in different ways. The simplest and "best" flaw is for something to simply not function at all while maintaining the underlying persistent access and command and control. For example, suppose there is a tool designed to hide files from the user. Sony famously installed such a tool in 2004 to protect a copy protection program surreptitiously installed by its music CDs. Among other functions, Sony's tool altered the operating system to hide all files that started with "sys". If there were a flaw, it would be better the tool simply failed to hide the files than to crash the operating system. In the first case, the user may not notice the extra files. In the second, the user will definitely notice their system crashing.

Worse than failing to function is a flaw that causes loss of access. However, as long as the user or administrator remains unaware, the operation is recoverable if the right contingency plans are in place.

The worst flaws are ones that cause a noticeable side effect. Noticeable effects can range from the innocuous, such as a temporary slowdown of connectivity, to the disastrous, such as repeatedly crashing a computer.

The Alureon rootkit of 2010 did exactly that after one particular Windows update.[4] This caused the rootkit to gain widespread attention, never a good thing for an attack tool.

In general, the severity of flaws depends on the Defender's reaction and not on the flaw itself. One of the enduring dishonors of the computer industry is that people have come to expect them to fail. And so they may not notice when something different is wrong. So the Attacker loses nothing. If, however, the Defender goes searching for a problem, as was the case when Stuxnet started crashing computers, then millions of dollars and months or perhaps years of effort can suddenly go down in flames.

Given the imperfect nature of software development, flawed software will remain a friction of CNE. The operational and program damage caused by this friction can range from inconsequential to catastrophic.

Upgrades and Updates

As detailed in Chapter 4, "Asymmetries," Defenders control the terrain. They can change the technical field at any time, for any reason, subject to their own economic constraints. There are many potential reasons: a company merger, opening a new office, integrating systems with a vendor, and so forth, but two types of changes are routine: upgrades and updates.

An *upgrade* introduces a new technology or substantially replaces an existing one. The previous technology is completely removed. You upgrade your phone or your car when you trade in the old one and get something different. Examples of upgrades include adding a new firewall, replacing a server, installing a different or completely new version of an operating system, or swapping a backup system from using tape backups to using off-site data transfer. In each case, the Attacker must discover and deal with something new.

An *update* is an improvement to something existing that leaves a substantial portion of the original in place. It is akin to getting new brakes and tires on your car. The new parts may be more efficient or effective, but they perform the same purpose as the ones they replaced. Updates mainly consist of installing newer versions of the same software.

The words *upgrade* and *update* are often used interchangeably, but there is an important operational nuance. Upgrades constitute a substantial threat to maintaining access for the Attacker. Access to the network can be lost when a firewall is installed or a server is replaced. The method for retrieving data may be eliminated when the backup system is swapped out.

Upgrades may challenge the Attacker's methods of persistence; for example, all persistent software is erased if you cleanly upgrade from Windows XP to Windows 7 64-bit. This includes all Attacker backdoors. And just like that, access to that computer disappears. Upgrades can be existential threats.

By contrast, updates are less ruinous. When Attackers establish access, they intentionally hook into areas of the network and systems that are unlikely to change. Updating from Mac OSX 10.8 to OSX 10.9 leaves most existing software, hopefully including Attacker software, in place. Nor does updating the version of Microsoft Office change how and where documents may be accessed. Updates may indeed cause problems, but they are rarely catastrophic, and they are generally problems that can be worked around on short notice.

Yet, no matter the effect and the difficulty of adjusting, neither updates nor upgrades are under the Attacker's control and are therefore a friction. Together these changes introduce a degree of uncertainty into the operation.

Other Attackers

It's happened to everyone who has ever been single. You meet an attractive woman or man, and the first thing you think is, "She's (he's) probably already taken." Why? Because you know that if you find this person attractive, other people do as well, and there's a good chance someone else has beat you to the punch.

Well, if the target network is attractive to one Attacker, it is probably already taken. If it is of interest to one, it is of interest to many. Further, by the same logic, if one Attacker can gain access, then others most certainly can as well. (And this doesn't include when Attackers piggyback on each other's access, like the NSA allegedly did to South Korea to gain access to North Korean systems.)[5] In other words: you are not alone.

Having multiple Attackers creates issues. The multiple offensive competencies and weaknesses become chained together. And you know the old adage about chain strength: the operational security of every Attacker is only as good as the least capable one. If one rogue Attacker triggers the alarms, then everyone gets caught up in the resulting sweep.

Consider the offensive organization dubbed "Equation Group" detailed in a report by Kaspersky in February 2015. In answer to the question "How did you discover this malware?" the report notes that it was not found directly, rather:

> We discovered one of the first EQUATIONDRUG modules during our research into the Regin nation-state APT operation. Somewhere in the Middle East, there is a computer we are calling the "The Magnet of Threats" because in addition to Regin, it was also infected by Turla, ItaDuke, Animal Farm and Careto/Mask. When we tried to analyze the Regin infection on this computer, we identified another module which did not appear to be part of the Regin infection, nor any of the other APTs.[6]

In addition to the most recently discovered Attacker, the "The Magnet of Threats" is running malware attributed to the United States, Russia, China, an unknown actor, and Spain, respectively. It's quite the popular machine. And collectively that popularity doomed all of the offensive players.

With multiple tool chains installed, it's a wonder the machine continued to run. That's because offensive tools may conflict. There are but so many ways to write a keystroke logger, for example, and many require modifying specific components of the operating system. Another Attacker's version may make unknown changes to a component your tool expects to behave a certain way. Perhaps one Attacker's tool simply supplants the other, or worse, together they make the keyboard stop working entirely. Testing with known software is hard enough. Assuring compatibility with unknown and often unstable-by-nature software is practically impossible.

Tradecraft may also conflict. For example, suppose the Defender monitors the amount of outgoing data. Individually each Attacker might be below the threshold, but together they could trigger an alert.

This is why Attackers need a defensive component as part of their forward-deployed tool kit. It's why the TDL4 rootkit removes other botnets.[7] It's why the Conficker worm patches the vulnerability it uses to gain access.[8] It removes competition for the same data, prevents someone else's actions from drawing attention, and eliminates potential incompatibilities. This kind of "offensive" defense is an all-around win for the Attacker.

But sometimes there's nothing you can do. Rogue Attackers do not even need to be after the same target to cause problems. They may just be using the same vulnerability or operational technique somewhere else. If caught, the capability is lost to everyone.

And this is in the best case, in which one assumes the rogue Attacker does not want to get caught. This is often untrue. Independent hacking groups crave attention. For example, consider the compromise of Syrian President Bashar al-Assad's e-mail:

> *Activists say they were able to monitor the inboxes of Assad and his wife in real time for several months. In several cases they claim to have used information to warn colleagues in Damascus of imminent regime moves against them.*
>
> *The access continued until 7 February, when a threatening email arrived in the inbox thought to be used by Assad after the account's existence was revealed when the Anonymous group separately hacked into a number of Syrian government email addresses. Correspondence to and from the two addresses ceased on the same day.[9]*

This is a clear demonstration of an operation gone wrong. The actions of a rogue Attacker compromised a source of intelligence for the Syrian opposition. In the end, Anonymous probably cost people's lives no matter its intent.

The presence of additional Attackers introduces an operational friction. It's yet another element the Attacker cannot control. Because multiple entities find the same type of information attractive, this friction will occur frequently.

The Security Community

The security community can create frictions in operations in two different ways: by strengthening defense or by weakening offense.

The first, and perhaps most obvious method, is to strengthen defenses via the sudden introduction of a new heuristic detection technique. The new heuristic may not even address something inherently malicious, just something that security companies notice only bad things do.

Consider a contrived example. Imagine that an Attacker has a program that searches a hard drive for documents. Searching in and of itself is not enough to label a program suspicious. A lot of programs search hard drives. iTunes searches computers for music files when it is first installed. Searchlight on Mac and the old Microsoft Indexing Service on Windows traverse the filesystem to build an index to speed user searches. Users may run "find" from the command line—the list goes on.

However, perhaps this Attacker program's search is slightly different. It searches only for Microsoft Word documents, opens them, reads the first page, and closes them. If no other software does this, then this sequence is a behavioral signature. The security community could push out an update that watches for this behavior and quarantines the offending programs.

Note that defensive security products themselves are not frictions. Only the new features are and then only for a short time. The development and deployment of a new version is entirely predictable, and once released, testable. If the company wants to make money, then it is out in the world marketing its product. Specific features or techniques may be hidden, but the existence of the product most certainly is not. The products are obstacles, not frictions, as some level of planning can be done to counteract them.

The second way the security community creates friction is through the independent discovery and publication of vulnerabilities and offensive techniques. This reaches in and pulls weapons out of the adversary's arsenal. This is the idea behind efforts such as Google Project Zero—find and fix vulnerabilities that either Attackers are keeping secret or haven't discovered yet.

(There is a philosophical debate over how vulnerabilities should be disclosed. Some argue that the vendor should be alerted and given time to develop a fix before the general public is notified. This is called "responsible disclosure." Others believe that this process is often too slow and it is better to warn customers immediately about the threat, but will hold back some technical details to avoid tipping off Attackers. Still others will just release full technical details and sample code to the world either not caring about the consequences or believing that a working demonstration is the only thing that will spur vendors to act.)

No matter how and when security vulnerabilities are disclosed, proactive discovery for updatable systems eventually makes the product more secure.

Even if the system cannot be updated, at least the defense has the chance to find a mitigation. The assumption that Attackers won't find vulnerabilities if they are kept secret is glaringly naïve when you accept that Attackers are both motivated and well funded.

The publication of offensive methods is as much a friction as other Attackers. The offense has to consider that at any given moment, anything they use could become public and disappear.

The security community is a source of friction, but much as it tries, it is not an existential threat. This is due to one unfortunate reality: the world is producing new insecure code and systems far faster than it is fixing the existing ones. Until this trend is reversed, the security community will remain a surmountable friction.

Bad Luck

Bad luck is the catchall for unnamed frictions. Perhaps there is a hardware failure in the target infrastructure on the single point of access. Perhaps someone goes on vacation for a month and shuts off her computer. Maybe the network connection fails at the exact moment an exploit is launched and causes the target machine to crash rather than be compromised.

It is impossible to enumerate everything that can go wrong, but no matter how much effort and planning goes into an operation, things will break. Murphy's law is always a factor.

Summary

The effect of frictions can be reduced through expertise, training, process, and technologies, but the frictions themselves can never be eliminated. In operations, as in life, there are always unplanned setbacks. Any coherent strategy must accommodate what a former U.S. Secretary of Defense would call these "known unknown" hindrances.[10]

Of course, unknown setbacks are not limited to one side. In the next chapter, we'll explore frictions that thwart the Defender.

Defender Frictions

It is possible to commit no mistakes and still lose.

—Captain Jean-Luc Picard

Defenders have their own set of impediments that occur repeatedly. At the top of the list is that they are consistently hacked, but stating this truth as a friction is not very helpful. What are some of the reoccurring issues that make defense more difficult? Identifying these and minimizing their effects is a must for any effective defensive strategy.

Mistakes

The Defender is human and therefore makes mistakes. Assuming the existence of a mistake-free environment can be your first mistake.

Not all mistakes are created equal. Accidentally leaving your workstation logged in while you go to lunch is a security issue, but unless someone walks by at that exact moment and installs something malicious, then it's a harmless mistake.

Other mistakes may be caught and corrected before it's too late. A Goldman Sachs contractor accidentally e-mailed "highly confidential" account information to someone's @gmail.com account instead of the @gs.com account that was intended. Sure they had to pay a lawyer to get a court order to get Google to delete the e-mail, but what could have been a breach of security was caught and fixed in time.[1]

Some mistakes have actual consequences. Misconfigure a firewall and suddenly the world can access the internal network. And access it they will. Fail to notice an alert, and what could have been an easily cordoned breach turns into millions of lost credit card numbers. This is the mistake the retailer Target committed in 2014.

The story [sources] tell is of an alert system, installed to protect the bond between retailer and customer, that worked beautifully. But then, Target stood by as 40 million credit card numbers—and 70 million addresses, phone numbers, and other pieces of personal information—gushed out of its mainframes.[2]

In January 2014, the Chinese Great Firewall started redirecting millions of users to Dynamic Internet Technology, a company that sells anticensorship software for Chinese users.[3] Oops! I would not want to be the guy who caused that. No doubt what we view as ironic, the Chinese government considered a critical security mistake.

The severity of a mistake's consequences depends on several factors, but a key one is whether a system is designed to fail "open" or fail "secure," where failure in this case means human error or oversight. Put another way: does a mistake leave things more accessible than wanted or less?

Failing to add a new user is a mistake, but one that fails secure. Failing to remove a user is a similar mistake, but that error fails open, leaving an avenue for unauthorized access. For security, the trick is to minimize the number of potential systems and processes that fail open and to develop a response plan for those that remain.

No matter how well prepared the Defender may be, mistakes and their effects are a key defensive friction.

Flawed Software

The Defender must deal with flawed software just like the Attacker. This much is obvious or security would be perfect, and offensive and defensive strategies would be irrelevant. Software is demonstrably flawed in all kinds of ways.

Software may be flawed in implementation, usually called a bug. The word *bug* simply means that a system has some behavior not intended by its developers. It may be that a particular program crashes if you try to open a menu while it is processing. It could be a truncated document causes the program to corrupt its own memory. It may be that the program *deadlocks*, a condition in which different parts of a program are waiting on each other so that nothing ever completes. (This is sometimes what causes your mouse cursor to change into a spinning wheel.) It could be the program fails to clean up nicely, slowly bringing the entire system to a halt. The list of bug manifestations goes on and on.

Software may be flawed by design. Do a search for "hardcoded backdoor," and you can find lists of printers, routers, and software from Samsung, Dell,

Barracuda, Netis, Cisco, and more where developers left in backdoors that require minimal skill to exploit. Even one of the FBI's wiretapping tools is vulnerable.[4]

Other flawed designs are not so egregious but involve flawed assumptions. For example, many industrial control system devices make the implicit assumption that they would never be connected to an externally accessible network. This was a reasonable assumption, especially since in many cases, at the time of initial development, the Internet did not exist yet. Fast-forward 10 or 20 years and someone bolts on a networking capability for remote management without reconsidering the consequences. There is no bug here. The system is performing exactly as intended and built. Yet it is hopelessly insecure.

Software may also be flawed by functional omission, meaning some feature or protection that should be there is not. Until September 2014, Apple's automatic mobile phone backup service, iCloud, allowed repeated failed login attempts with no consequences. To the dismay of many female Hollywood celebrities, this functional oversight allowed hackers to try millions of passwords, eventually logging in to the accounts by brute force. Once in, they restored the celebrity's phone backups to their own devices, downloading several intimate photographs in the process. Apple's security model was not broken, nor was there a bug. But its security failure by omission, and then quite a bit more, was laid bare for all to see.

Even security software is not immune. A quick search of the Common Vulnerabilities and Exposure's database maintained by the U.S. government shows that between 6/2014 and 9/2014, a short 3-month time window, the security products companies Kaspersky, Symantec, McAfee, AVG, Panda Security, Cisco, and Juniper all had reported vulnerabilities in at least one of their products. Some created additional attack vectors that would not have been there if the product were not installed.

There is nothing special about the preceding company list or the time frame. Searching for practically any security company yields results, if not in those 3 months, then within the last year. Security vendors have every motivation to make products secure, but they, too, release flawed technology.

In short, regardless of intent or resources, decades of experience have taught us that all software has flaws and some percentage of those flaws affect security. So what can be done?

Simply removing flawed software is impractical. Even if flawed software could be recognized (all evidence suggests it can't), you cannot remove anything the Defender depends on even if it is egregiously insecure.

Upgrading may not be an option either. The original software developer may be out of business. It may be an embedded system that cannot be updated. It may be so intertwined into the call center, manufacturing equipment, inventory tracking, or other business critical system as to be unrealistic to replace. Upgrading, even when technically possible, may be simply cost prohibitive.

Patching is its own friction. Figure 6.1 shows what patching is like for one computer.

Figure 6.1: All Adobe Updates[5]

The potential confusion and frustration is only multiplied in a corporate environment. The Defender must not only spend time and resources applying patches as they arise, but they must also spend precious time proactively testing updates lest they negatively impact the business. Or instead they must respond to any applied updates that break things.

Broken updates are not a theoretical issue. The September 2014 update to iOS 8.0.1 for iPhone prevented many devices from, well, working as a phone. It killed the ability to get cellular service. Not 1 month earlier Microsoft released an update that caused many Windows systems to crash. And these updates are from well-funded companies.

Whether by implementation, design, or omission, flawed software is here to stay. In some cases, it cannot be updated, but even in those where it can, the updated versions will contain flaws. In the best case, these flaws will serve as a source of negligible unpredictability to the Defender; in the worst, a source of entry or expansion for the Attacker. They are an irremovable defensive friction.

Inertia

Law I. Every body perseveres in its state of rest, or of uniform motion in a right line, unless it is compelled to change that state by forces impressed thereon.

—Sir Isaac Newton from *Philosophiæ Naturalis Principia Mathematica*

Newton's First Law of Motion, or the law of inertia, is one of the foundations of physics. But it should be considered a foundation to human psychology and action as well.

Consider Windows XP. It is well over a decade old and has not been supported since April 2014. It is by definition insecure now, as every new vulnerability discovered will be permanent. It's not as if the original software developer went out of business. There is a replacement readily available, and Microsoft has expended untold effort to ensure Windows 7 and 8 are backward compatible.

Still XP persists in the millions. Why? Inertia: it requires "force" to change, where force is the resources and motivation to change and the knowledge that it is necessary.

The cost of upgrading is clear. It takes time and expertise to do the upgrade, money for the new operating system, and money to replace old hardware. It may also take time, expertise, and money to deal with any resulting incompatibilities.

What's the cost of not upgrading? At some point in the near or distant future, an Attacker may or may not get access to this computer, and then do something that may or may not cause anyone any heartache whatsoever. Tough choice? Not really. The system works. Leave it alone and go concentrate on something else.

This, of course, assumes people are even making that choice. Most people have automatic updates set for their computers, but how many people know if the firmware on their home router is up to date? How many know what firmware is? (It's the low-level software burned into the device that loads the operating system.) What are the risks if it is out of date? Answer: who cares? People have better things to worry about. They are quite justifiably ignorant, and this ignorance is a form of inertia.

Inertia is hard to overcome. "If it ain't broke, don't fix it" is a perfectly rational attitude, especially when fixing it requires time and money. Sometimes even "Well it is broke, but fixing it would be hard" wins the day as well. Google aptly demonstrated this attitude with a January 2015 announcement that they will not fix security issues in WebView, a component currently on 60% of Android phones.[6] Even multibillion dollar companies have levels of inertia they are unwilling to overcome.

Until the cost of not upgrading is made more painful than neglecting other duties, inertia will remain a defensive friction.

The Security Community

The security community seeks out flaws to get them addressed. As discussed earlier, this is a clear Attacker friction. So how does discovery hurt the Defense?

What if a Defender cannot update due to incompatibilities or because the flaw is built into the hardware? Even if they could update, inertia and resource constraints may prevent all Defenders from updating in a timely fashion.

On July 16, 2003, Microsoft released a patch for a vulnerability in Windows (MS 03-2026). Prior to this, as far as anyone knows, no one outside of Microsoft was aware of the issue. By July 25th, the Chinese group xFocus reverse engineered the patch to discover the vulnerability and published a proof of concept on how to exploit it. By August 11th, a worm was found spreading on the Internet. By August 15th, the now named Blaster Worm had infected more than 400,000 computers. As shown in the time line in Figure 6.2, that's less than one month from a released patch to a widespread worm.

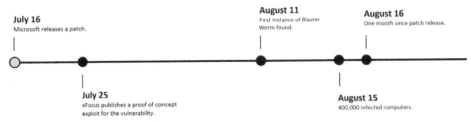

Figure 6.2: Blaster Worm time line

The Attacker was handed a new attack vector by the patch. What could Microsoft have done differently? Nothing. Microsoft's actions improved security in the long run. The alternative of not releasing the patch would have left everyone insecure, not to mention exposing the company to untold liability.

For a more recent example, in September 2014, a critical flaw in the Linux program Bash was disclosed by Red Hat, a Linux development and support company. The Linux operating system powers more than one-half the world's websites, and Bash is a key component of almost every Linux system.

At the same time the flaw was disclosed, a fix was released. The fix itself was incomplete, but that did not actually matter. Within 24 hours, Attackers were actively scanning the Internet and using the vulnerability in the wild. Let me repeat: attacks were detected within 24 hours, a next-to-impossible deadline for any IT staff.

These are but two examples. Many smaller, less widespread flaws are reported all the time. In some cases, because they are less popular, they do not receive as much attention, and therefore Defenders are even more likely to delay or forgo updating.

In finding flaws and fixing them, the security community can make the Attackers' job paradoxically easier. The security community is therefore a source of friction to Defenders.

Complexity

Every technical aspect of the target is complex. Computers and networks are complicated things. They have architectures, operating systems, file systems, protocols, applications, and more. Typical users scratch only the surface of understanding the components that sit on their desks. My laptop has 400,000+ files and 50+ programs running on it when it first starts up. Which are necessary? Which have vulnerabilities? There is simply no way to tell. It is far too complicated. And that's only the computer in front of me.

The backbone of any network, the routers, are complex computers that are less visible, but equally vulnerable. Until recently, few paid any attention to these devices, but that changed in 2014 when a worm was released for Linksys routers, a prolific home brand.[7] This particular worm, dubbed "TheMoon," was not very effective, but it could have been. Time and money is all that stood between a somewhat harmless annoyance and a full-featured home router toolkit that could redirect online banking, eavesdrop on insecure communications, or serve as an entry point into the network behind it.

Practically every network in the world also contains a printer. The dot matrix printers of yore were pretty simple, but a modern printer runs a full operating system. In September 2014, a researcher compromised a Canon Pixma printer and reprogrammed it to play the legendary game Doom on its tiny LCD screen.[8] Does anyone doubt he could have instead surreptitiously copied and exfiltrated every printed document? Modern printer complexity makes them ripe for exploitation.

Given that printer flaws have been demonstrated for years now, I am surprised that my searches turn up no real-world examples of printer malware. Of course, this may have more to do with the fact that few, if any, defensive tools exist. If your printer was infected, how would you know? Answer: you wouldn't.

In 2000, Bruce Schneier wrote in his book *Secrets and Lies*, "Complexity is the worst enemy of security. . . . A more complex system is less secure on all fronts. It contains more weaknesses to start with, it's modularity exacerbates those weaknesses, it's harder to test, it's harder to understand, and it's harder to analyze."[9]

I'll add one more to the list: it's harder to fix, even if the vulnerability is understood. When, for example, Microsoft identifies, analyzes, and develops a fix for a security issue, it still has to retest it on thousands of operating system configurations, and despite best efforts, the fix is sometimes flawed.

In November 2014, Microsoft pushed out a patch for the SChannel flaw, a serious remote execution vulnerability affecting all versions of Windows since 2003. For some, the patch caused processes to hang, services to become unresponsive, issues with certain database applications, and more.[10] Microsoft had to retract the patch and issue another one a couple weeks later. Microsoft, a company with years of experience testing and issuing patches, missed the complex interactions the first time around.

The same problem exists for any major software vendor. Fixing complex systems is more costly and adds to the difficulty of defense.

Complexity also makes deployment mistakes more likely. Even if all software were flaw free in terms of vulnerabilities, it still requires someone to configure and use it. A firewall with a single misconfiguration can turn an otherwise impervious fortress into a Maginot Line.

Finally, complexity is hard to avoid. Witness the recently developed U.S. government system for purchasing health care insurance, also known as Healthcare.gov. Unsubstantiated reports put it in the 3 million lines of code range for the site and all its various backend systems, databases, and interchanges. This number may or may not be true, but it's reasonable enough.

And that's the scary part: 3 million lines of code are reasonable for the scope of what needed to be accomplished. How many people believe that this system was adequately security tested before launch? While contemplating your answer, keep in mind it was not adequately *functionally* tested before launch. You might then ask, why was it so complicated? For the same reason most software is complicated. It's the only way to deliver the features that the market, or in this case the law, demanded.

(By the way, lest you think this is a political commentary, I would be far more concerned about the 100s of millions of lines of code in the operating systems, databases, and network infrastructure that this and every other public service runs on top of. Oh, that and the insurance companies with actual medical information, not just eligibility information, that have already been hacked. The latest example is the insurance giant Anthem who, almost as if on cue, had 80 million customer records stolen in early 2015, corresponding to tens of millions of customers.[11])

On top of all this, not only is complexity hard to avoid creating, it's hard to simplify once created.

> *The Department of Veterans Affairs and the Department of Defense spent at least $1.3 billion during the last four years trying unsuccessfully to develop a single electronic health-records system between the two departments—leaving veterans' disability claims to continue piling up in paper files across the country, a News21 investigation shows.*
>
> *This does not include billions of other dollars wasted during the last three decades, including $2 billion spent on a failed upgrade to the DOD's existing electronic health-records system.[12]*

Attempting to combine and simplify two military systems was a complete failure. Starting from scratch is not necessarily much better either. Witness the Virtual Case File, a program designed to replace the FBI's legacy Automated Case Support system: 170 million dollars later, the new system was abandoned entirely.

There's certainly plenty of blame to go around in every example of failed attempts to reduce complexity, and rest assured, fingers get pointed in all directions by a lot of people. However, these are just a small sample of the highly publicized ones. The larger point remains: complexity is the worst enemy of security, and it is not going anywhere. It is a friction for every aspect of defensive security.

Users

A great source of friction for the Defender is the user base. Users will ignore policy. They will find a way to undo security restrictions that they find cumbersome. They will ignore warning signs of compromise and chalk it up to "that's just what the computer does sometimes."

Users will open unsolicited attachments. They will forward company proprietary information to their own web mail accounts. Even seemingly innocuous behavior, like bringing in a child's book report on a thumb drive for printing, can cause security headaches.

I have witnessed an employee bring in hard drives full of music and movies (and whatever malware may have gotten on to them) and connect the drives to the company network. Another hooked up a computer outside the company firewall to circumvent restrictions on downloads. The funny part is neither act was malicious. In the download case, there was actually a legitimate business reason for it. Yet neither user bothered to clear the insecure behavior through IT.

There is no end to the creative abuse that the user base can and will find. And this assumes no malice whatsoever.

What is the best way to deal with this? The security-conscious network administrator walks a fine line. Imposing strict controls without the ability to quickly deal with the inevitable exceptions just breeds a hostile user base. Imagine having to put in a request to browse the results of a Google search. I've seen one company try this. The rule lasted less than a day. Employees do not like to wait minutes, never mind hours or days, to gain access to something they feel is justified. The Internet is full of stories where employees feel that corporate IT just gets in the way.

Also, what should an administrator do when the "stupid user" who causes issues is the boss? According to one survey of security professionals by ThreatTrack Security, 40% of respondents said they "had to remove malware after a senior executive visited an infected pornographic website."[13] I have to believe most executives were warned not to browse porn at work at some point in their careers. And still, 40%.

So what's the right course of action here? Attempt to restrict his access to contain the damage or quietly let it pass and just deal with it? Making the correct security call should not involve weighing your career prospects, but in the real world it can.

There is no easy win with users. Short of introducing draconian consequences, the user base will ignore good practice and policy when it suits them and therefore will always remain a Defender friction.

Bad Luck

Murphy's law is not limited to the Attacker. Laptops will be stolen. Disgruntled employees will retaliate. Servers will suffer inopportune outages. Software that worked for years will stop working because of some unrelated update. The Defender's attention will be grabbed and held elsewhere to the detriment of security.

Not every friction can be named, predicted, or planned for despite all care. Bad luck will always play a role.

Summary

The effect of frictions can be reduced through expertise, training, process, and technologies, but the frictions themselves can never be eliminated. Both Attacker and Defender must craft a strategy that recognizes and accommodates their frictions while seeking to increase those of their opponent.

In the next chapter, we'll explore the framework of offensive principles necessary to maximize offensive asymmetric advantages and minimize frictions.

Offensive Strategy

*If you don't know where you are going,
any road will get you there.*

—Lewis Carroll

What is a strategy? It is a plan for achieving a specific goal, that which connects the ends to the means.

Strategy is in contrast to tactics, the specific actions taken during the plan's execution. In football (or basketball or soccer), strategy is developing the playbook. Tactics are calling the play. Strategy is determining which players to draft. Tactics are picking who starts a particular game.

The two terms are often used interchangeably, and admittedly, the differences can be clouded. But in CNE, there is a clear demarcation line: the moment the Attacker attempts to gain initial access. *Strategy* is everything done in preparation for this moment and the resulting operational life cycle. *Tactics* embody the execution after this moment.

Why does defining this line matter? Because it forces you to look beyond the tactic of the moment, the thing that will be irrelevant 6 months from now, and ask questions like, "What training programs should be developed?" or "Where is redundancy necessary and where is it wasteful?" These are important questions to answer to build a program of operations, and they are above individual tactics.

Crafting a successful strategy requires a clearly defined goal. As detailed in Chapter 2, "The Attacker," CNE goals are human in nature. With Stuxnet, the goal was the frustration of the Iranian nuclear program. With the attack on Sony Pictures, the real goal was not to prevent the release of a movie, but rather to send the geopolitical message "We have the ability to damage your companies and your economy." The motive behind Target or Home Depot? Money. The goal of compromising the U.S. State Department e-mail system?[1] Intelligence.

The goals vary widely, but each is achieved through five well-defined operational objectives: strategic collection, directed collection, non-kinetic computer network attack, strategic access, and positional access, which in turn all require the same foundational means: sustained undetected access.

Crafting a successful strategy requires embracing the fundamental truths of the space. The three foundational principles of humanity, access, and economy form these truths. These laws are like the laws of physics. They guide everything, and if you understand them, they provide a base of power.

Crafting a successful strategy requires determining and reducing the uncertainty of frictions while increasing those of one's opponent. If every mistake you make or every update has the potential to cause operational failure, then your strategy is flawed.

Finally, crafting a successful strategy requires determining and maximizing advantageous asymmetries, while minimizing those of your opponent. Sony is in the business of making movies, and the resulting lack of focus on network security is an enormous offensive advantage.

So it's clear there is a list of things any successful strategy must have. But how do you gauge the effectiveness of a specific potential strategy? How can you measure whether something is likely to succeed or fail when so much is uncertain? You do this by developing a framework of principles and measuring how a strategy stacks up against the ideal. The following ideas outlined in Figure 7.1 form the foundation of such a framework for CNE.

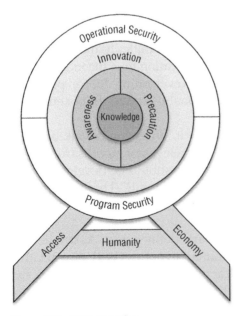

Figure 7.1: CNE principles

Principle 1: Knowledge

Knowledge is the in-depth understanding of the technical aspects of architecture, operating systems, networks, and so on as well as understanding the psychological aspects of people and organizations. Knowledge is target agnostic and acquired outside of any specific operation.

Knowledge is essential to leverage all three foundational principles for operational success.

Technical knowledge makes more economical use of limited resources. For example, knowledge of standard network setups can speed target expansion. It can fill in gaps in target awareness (more on that later). Knowledge of memory architectures and specific exploit methodologies can make the difference between a theoretical vulnerability and gaining target access. Technical knowledge is often the only answer to technical constraints.

Psychological knowledge enables the Attacker to leverage the foundational principle of humanity and to predict Defender actions. It enables people to craft better social engineering lures and to understand when hiding in plain sight is a better strategy than technical stealth.

Business and social knowledge enables the Attacker to determine the points of access. It focuses the Attacker on the methods of access that must be left open for an organization to function. Cultural knowledge can affect the entire plan of operations.

This list goes on. With knowledge, there is no limit to the potential improvements in productivity.

Knowledge also reduces frictions. Knowledge of solid software development methods helps reduce flawed attack tools. It warns when updates are coming, how products work, when a particular operational technique is burned, or how to stay concealed from or in harmony with other Attackers.

Any offensive strategy must be measured by how effectively it will obtain, organize, and leverage knowledge. Yet there is a cost that must be considered. Acquiring knowledge requires time and money, whether formal training, buying books, or reverse engineering some new defensive security application. Time spent acquiring unused knowledge is effectively wasted. That time and money could have been better spent pursuing other objectives.

Knowledge also has limits. Knowledge bases in the real world are generally incomplete and frequently inaccurate. Most often they are a combination of both. Relying on the theoretical is a recipe for failure.

Further, no single individual is an expert in all things, and their biases are exacerbated by their field of knowledge. When confronted with a problem, a software engineer will want to design a program, the hardware engineer a device, and the operator will want to just use duct tape and gum and move forward. The old adage "If all you have is a hammer, everything looks like a nail" applies. Knowledge determines what kind of hammer you carry.

Consider a "computer geek," steeped in technological knowledge but ignorant of social psychology. While the Hollywood stereotype may be extreme, some organizations exhibit traits of the caricature. On one extreme, the superior technical knowledge leads to arrogance and an air of invincibility. No one could possibly understand what he's doing, never mind catch him. The Attacker becomes careless.

One the other extreme, the Attacker becomes paranoid, fixating on all the ways to get caught. This person can think of everything possible that can go wrong. He considers every possible countermeasure, regardless of likelihood. As each possible method of failure is contemplated, risk aversion seeps in and total paralysis ensues. In this case, a more technologically ignorant Attacker might actually be more successful.

The best decisions are made by those that have a balance of knowledge of the technical, psychological, and social aspects of operations.

Measuring Knowledge

How can you balance the costs of acquiring and maintaining knowledge with the benefits it brings, while acknowledging its limitations? In the end, *knowledge improves operational efficiency and effectiveness.*

Therefore, the Attacker must identify those aspects of operations that occur frequently enough that they are worth investing the time to learn up front versus those that can be learned if and when needed.

A simple rule of thumb: leaders' knowledge should be diverse. It should be acquired breadth first. Leaders should feel comfortable understanding both the technical and nontechnical risks in a given scenario. They should understand high-level network architecture and the corporate structure that dictates and maintains it. Time should be invested in understanding the art of the possible over the specifics of how to do it.

As for the attack team, the balance will depend on the mission and the frequency of similar operations. Diversity may be important for attacking a university, which may contain a physics department running HP-UX, a staff services network running Windows, and a chemistry department filled with Macs. All these may be of interest, or perhaps only as stepping stones to the real target: the research hospital running Linux. That said, depth of knowledge may reign supreme for specialized targets, such as a nuclear fission program with embedded controllers.

In crafting and evaluating a strategy, Attackers must contemplate their mission objectives, internal makeup, resources, and other factors and then invest in the people, technologies, and training necessary for acquiring, organizing, and accessing requisite knowledge.

In my experience, you are doing things right if, when needed, you can find or create a field expert in less than two months.

Principle 2: Awareness

Awareness is the careful mapping of the operational domain as well as the active detection and passive monitoring of events in near real time. Unlike knowledge, awareness is gleaned from the target environment and is *target specific.*

Awareness seeks to counteract the Defender's asymmetrical advantage of turf control. If you know the network as well as the Defender, or even better, then you have more options.

I once saw a network where the production servers were essentially unassailable from the outside. They had properly configured firewalls in place, rigorous monitoring, and strong access controls. They did everything right. Well, almost everything. With careful surveying, we became aware that there was another network, a staging network, where every production server was set up and configured before deployment into the hardened environment.

This staging network was all but open. This realization made the solution trivial: hit a new server during setup, and then sit back and wait as it is pulled back behind the walls. The parallel to the Trojan horse was deliciously literal. Sure, the window of opportunity was typically less than one day, but that was more than enough with proper awareness.

Through awareness the Attacker learns which machines are routinely logged in to by administrators, which systems are most heavily scrutinized, which users have the most technical issues, how data is backed up, and other points of interest or potential pitfalls.

Awareness may allow the Attacker to discern when the frictions of updates and upgrades are coming or where they will be deployed. For example, the Attacker may notice that scheduled downtime for updates occurs the first Saturday of every month. This gives fair warning as to when network changes can be expected. Then, if something changes out of schedule it's a signal. If machines start unexpectedly updating, then perhaps the Attacker has been discovered. Now might be a good time to go read the CSO's e-mail to find out why.

The human aspects of awareness may tell the Attacker the likelihood and consequences of being caught. I once went into an Internet café in a Middle Eastern country where the home page of Internet Explorer, the default web browser, was set to a porn site. Security was clearly not a priority here. On a corporate network, porn not only indicates poor security, but it creates a social barrier to offering up the computer for inspection. Both work to the Attacker's advantage and can guide which tools the Attacker chooses to deploy.

Awareness leads to the more effective deployment of tactics. For example, the Attacker may learn to employ more stealth on certain highly monitored systems, or to avoid them entirely. Awareness of purchase requests can tell you when a new firewall has been ordered, or how the company is migrating their database servers to Oracle. Or it may direct the Attacker into building redundant access into a new network segment while the one of primary interest is undergoing updates. Awareness ensures these tactical measures are judiciously leveraged.

Full awareness and a corresponding ability to quickly react would make it virtually impossible for the Attacker to be detected or removed from the network. Attackers simply tailor their tools to the threat, remove them, go silent, or employ any number of tactics as needed.

However, where there is a cost associated with obtaining knowledge, there is operational risk with acquiring awareness. Each data point can be acquired only by collecting and exfiltrating information from the target, which requires running survey and collection tools and sending data out of the network for analysis. It requires the expansion of access to other portions of the network. Achieving awareness requires greater exposure and risk.

Too much awareness can also lead to overconfidence. A highly aware Attacker can grow complacent, making it possible for the first unanticipated Defender move to have devastating consequences. If the Defender always stages changes on a QA network, what happens the first time someone skips that step and deploys right to production?

Too much awareness can also be paralyzing. With too many dots, you can connect them to form any picture. Shadows emerge from the information. Because Attackers know their own moves, they grow to assume that every anomalous action may be noticed. To counter this mentality, Attackers must consider that they might actually be monitoring the network better than the Defender.

Measuring Awareness

What is the balance between awareness and the operational risk it entails? In the end, *awareness buys time*: time to innovate, time to put in redundancy, time to collect data, and potentially time to clean up and clear out. The Attacker's cleanup of Flame, a tool set analyzed in Chapter 9, "Offensive Case Studies," began *before* a signature was developed for it.

The Attacker's level of precaution (principle 4) and their reaction time are key factors in evaluating the awareness trade-off. The higher the level of precaution and the faster the reaction time, the less awareness that is required.

Awareness buys this extra time using analysis expertise, attack tool development, and operational risk as the currency. The measure of success is first, whether the Attacker maintains access and second, whether the time and money invested in capabilities is safeguarded in the event of detection.

Principle 3: Innovation

Innovation is the ability to create new technology, leverage existing technologies in new ways, or develop and adapt operational methods.

Innovation requires creativity. Creativity is essential for finding flaws by divining assumptions that engineers and administrators may have not realized they were making and then violating those assumptions. It's required for finding new ways to hide, to survey, or to move throughout a network.

Creativity is truly dangerous when combined with awareness and knowledge of humanity. For example, suppose there is outbound bandwidth monitoring on a network. Does that monitoring apply to the CEO? Maybe. That's worth determining. Can data be internally pushed to the web server and then pulled out via web browser requests thus avoiding the caps entirely? A creative Attacker can find these weaknesses and exploit them.

So why is the strategic principle *innovation* and not creativity? Simply put, a creative idea is worthless if poorly executed. Execution requires methodical exploration, expansion, development, and application of the idea. *Innovation is creativity brought to scale through sound engineering.*

Innovation can improve efficiencies and decrease frictions. Better technology development processes lead to more reliable software and hardware. This reduces the friction of flawed attack tools.

Through innovation, complex, repetitive, or time-consuming operational tasks can be automated. A network map can be built from a simple packet capture. Analysis can be visualized so that relationships and important information are readily identified. Knowledge and experience can be built into the Attacker's tools. Together these actions conserve resources and the precious commodity of time while decreasing mistakes.

Measuring Innovation

There is no downside to constant innovation beyond the resources it consumes. In a successful offensive strategy, the Attacker's key challenge is to establish and adjust the balance between the leaps of creativity and the solidification and scalability of those leaps accomplished via engineering. Even the best engineered solutions face problems in practice, and this must be accounted for.

In some cases, the Attacker may leach off others' innovation. The security community publishes new attack methods to warn people. The underground community does the same in an effort to abuse people. Attackers don't need to care about motives if piggybacking on others' efforts lower their own costs.

In fact, Attackers may choose to focus their innovation on esoteric areas, entrusting that the community will shoulder some of the burden on more widespread technologies. This conserves energy and increases capabilities. Finding the right level of innovation balance in an offensive strategy is no different than the decisions companies make about internal R&D budgets. The cost is evident whereas the rewards may not be, but it's also obvious that investing nothing in research will lead to failure.

Defensive Innovation

There are defensive innovations the Attacker must counter, and collectively, the defensive industry has enormous resources. But the industry has some challenges in bringing those resources to fruition effectively.

The foremost challenge is the historical apathy of the software industry. In general, security does not sell products. Further, there has been no legal liability for insecurity. If a GM car fails to stop because the ignition switch is defective, then (eventually) lawsuits are filed, hearings are held, and government penalties are levied. What recourse do you have if your computer crashes or a browser vulnerability leaks out your credit card information? Answer: none. What if your business strategy is leaked to a competitor? Who gets sued? Answer: no one.

With no liability it was (and unfortunately still is) perfectly rational for software vendors to deprioritize security. There was no financial upside and little downside. Security could always be bolted on later should the market demand it. And so they did.

Fast-forward a couple decades to now, and there is an enormous amount of insecure technology deployed. Some of that technology is no longer maintained and will never be updated. Some technology is maintained, but it's difficult to update. And some may be easy to update, but companies are driven by profits, and security fixes in old products do not drive profits.

And the problem continues. Consider Snapchat, a mobile app based on the idea of "secure" communications where the sender can control a sent message or photo after delivery. Their marketing stated that sent photos "disappear forever" despite several proven ways to prevent this. The result of the obvious discrepancy? The FTC got involved and settled through a consent decree whereby Snapchat agreed to change their marketing material and implement a privacy program. Annoying perhaps, but hardly punishing. Meanwhile users and investors hardly noticed. The company has a market capitalization of $19 billion as of 2015.

This history creates a problem for any kind of defensive innovation. Defensive software must be backward compatible with these insecure products even if they exhibit what are now considered suspicious characteristics. This is a tough balance for the defensive security community. Prevent all insecure behavior and there's the potential to annoy the user base or worse, stop businesses from running. When the software running your manufacturing plant, the NASDAQ, or your inventory system exhibits suspicious behavior, the only choice for a defensive product is to allow the behavior and put security at risk. The costs of interruption are simply too high.

A simple answer would be to replace every insecure product. But, consider the following thought experiment: Every known insecure product is replaced with something with no known issues. Does that make security perfect? No.

The key phrase is that there are no "known" issues, not "no" issues. There is no guarantee that security improved with the new version. Each year a newly minted batch of engineers enters the workforce ready to make the same mistakes as their predecessors or find entirely new ones to make on their own. The risk of introducing bugs increases with each new feature and each new level of complexity, and technology is getting more complex.

General apathy and lack of liabilities pretty much guarantees that each generation of defensive innovation will be met by a generation of new security weaknesses.

The asymmetry of *opponent analysis* is also a challenge to defensive innovation. It is difficult to develop countermeasures against unknown Attacker innovations. One solution is to innovate your own offensive methods and then preemptively build defenses. Indeed, this is what many individual researchers try to do. Unfortunately, this doesn't scale well in a for-profit business. Imagine telling your profit-driven manager, "I want to spend the next 3–6 months researching potential attacks and developing countermeasures for things that Attackers may never develop and our customers may never need." A certain amount of this may be tolerated as R&D, but it's not going to get the substantial resources it actually requires.

Defensive innovation is also hindered because defensive products are simply overwhelmed. It is enough work trying to block out the proverbial 98 percent of unskilled Attackers (that create millions of malware variants per year) that it is difficult to have time to focus on the 2 percent that are truly elite.

Yet, all this is not to say that defense cannot out innovate the offense. These challenges are surmountable, especially as the bandwidth, storage, and processing power available continue to increase. If the market begins to incentivize security, historical disadvantages will dissipate as old software is phased out. Already in the mobile computing arena, people have accepted decreased freedom of usage in exchange for a greater degree of security. Apple's devices are locked to only running vetted apps. Whether this is an acceptable trade for everyone does not diminish the success of the iPhone and App Store. If this trend extends into general-purpose computing, it may shift the balance.

Regardless, there will forever be a race between offensive and defensive innovation. In the end, *innovation confers a tactical advantage*. The Attacker must combine creativity with engineering to maintain this advantage. Due to historical circumstance, the Attacker begins the race with a lead, but as new technologies and platforms are developed, unless the Attacker remains focused on long-term innovation, that lead will disappear.

Principle 4: Precaution

Precaution is the minimization of the effect of *unwitting* actions on an operation.

Why unwitting? Because virtually all Defender actions are taken without knowledge of the Attacker's presence. People do their jobs, and for the most part, those jobs are unrelated to computer security. The company accounting, HR, sales, marketing, delivery, or engineering staff members simply do not contemplate how their online actions affect the Attacker. The only exception is when Defenders are actively trying to remove the Attacker. And in this case, either they will succeed and the operation will end, or they will fail and some part of the Attacker's operation will remain unknown.

Unwitting actions can get the Attacker caught. Perhaps one person decides to stay late. This simple change in routine may impact an operation if, for example, the Attacker regularly pulls out data after hours and the user notices and reports a slowdown in performance.

Unwitting actions can also impede operations. Perhaps a user changes a password that the Attacker relied upon. Or worse, perhaps the Attacker's primary point of access in the network is disconnected, formatted, and repurposed elsewhere. These are small-scale changes to the Defender's network, ones that do not require advance planning or warning, yet they may be catastrophic to the Attacker.

Unwitting actions are also not limited to those performed by people. Hardware fails all the time. There are power outages, air-conditioning overloads, upstream network service provider changes, and so on. These anomalies occur beyond what the Attacker can predict through knowledge and awareness. They are outside the control of both the Attacker and the Defender, but that does not stop them from causing Attacker disruptions.

Precaution is the strategic principle that fills the void left by the impossibility of obtaining total awareness. It guards against accidental disruptions. Precaution can take many forms, but there are two overriding themes: redundancy and diversity.

- **Redundancy** is establishing reasonable fail-safes, backups, and contingency plans for foreseeable setbacks or obstacles.
- **Diversity** is leveraging a wide range of tools, technologies, development methods, network signatures, infrastructure, and operational methods.

Sustaining access through unwitting changes can be achieved by establishing redundant points of access. Then if hardware fails on a single point, or if the operating system is reinstalled, or if Murphy's Law asserts itself in any one of a thousand ways, the operation continues to live. Redundancy removes the reliance on a particular computer or device remaining unperturbed.

But it is not good enough to just be redundant. Otherwise, whatever caused the failure of the first may impact the second. The redundancy must have independent modes of failure. Access methods must be diverse.

Implementing diversity helps prevent any one change from causing full operational failure. Even if each method or point of access is systematically closed off, there is often a time lag found in updating disparate systems that can be exploited to stay ahead of the shutdown wave.

For example, the Attacker may create points of access on different operating systems like Windows and Linux. That way an update applied to one will not affect the others, and there is time to regroup. If they are kicked off the Windows machines, then Attackers have time to reestablish themselves by launching from the Linux machines.

There is an added bonus to persisting on disparate platforms as well. An antivirus signature for Windows is not going to affect a Linux backdoor. Most security software is not cross platform, but even if it were, persistence methods are highly platform specific and therefore the tools that leverage them will have widely different signatures.

Attackers may also diversify the types of hardware they infect. Perhaps the embedded software on a network card is updated in case a hard drive goes bad. Maybe the Attacker persists on both the computers and the routers. When is the last time you updated the firmware on your printer? Answer: never.

Recently, it was discovered that one group, dubbed the Equation Group by Kaspersky, managed to persist in the firmware of a hard drive controller.[2] This capability is practically the definition of precaution. It survives the complete cleaning and reformatting of a computer. (Note: the malware itself was only discovered because the installer was found.)

The Attacker may also use a diversity of network protocols. Then, if the Defender installs an appliance to monitor web traffic, access via e-mail may still work. Or perhaps e-mail is monitored but no one looks at instant messaging.

Precaution is exercised in other parts of an operation beyond maintaining access as well. For example, during access expansion, the Attacker may consistently capture new passwords to prepare for when one changes. During data collection, the Attacker may make copies of the data on the target in case a poorly timed vacation renders the data inaccessible for retrieval.

Each of these actions prevents unwitting actions from impacting the operation.

Measuring Precaution

Precaution must be used judiciously. Too little precaution and luck is in charge of whether what otherwise would be a minor setback causes a failed operation. It is easy to grow lax while primary methods are working.

On the other end, too much precaution creates undue risk. Establishing redundant points of access creates a larger footprint to be noticed. For each exfiltration method, there is a corresponding list of ways to detect that method. Owning a network every way possible is a recipe for disaster.

What level of precaution is required for a given operation? In the end, *precaution protects against difficult-to-predict events that cause catastrophic consequences.*

It is like an insurance policy. And like insurance, the Attacker's goal is to minimize the amount of the investment while maximizing the dividend. So where does one draw the line?

For each network segment, a general rule is:

$$\text{Points of access per segment} = \text{natural\_log(number of devices)}$$

Table 7.1 shows a sample calculation for the number of points of access for a company with 1,000+ devices.

Table 7.1: Sample Calculation of Points of Access

SEGMENT	NUMBER OF DEVICES	POINTS OF ACCESS
DMZ	10	2
Human Resources	4	1
Users at main office	1,000	7
Remote users	100	4
IT	5	2 (special case)
Servers	20	3
Total	1,139	19

Of course the specific target situation must be taken into account. With 5 network administrators, I would want 2 points of access—unless there was a strong security posture. In that case, I would avoid the IT network entirely. Still, this formula serves as a good starting point.

It's not necessary to have presence on every computer, or even a constant fraction of devices. This quickly gets untenable as developing and maintaining this many points of access is not without cost. It requires a broader range of technical expertise, more analysts, more focus, and, of course, more time.

Instead, increasing the number of redundant points of access logarithmically provides a reasonable balance between resiliency and exposure, not to mention the amount of effort required to maintain each point.

Diversity of tools must also be balanced. Too little and a single network change can wipe out all access. Too much diversity and the Attacker's exposure is unduly increased. Every tool used is a risk. If caught, it not only puts the Defender on the hunt, but it has the potential to affect every other operation where that tool is used.

The ideal level of diversity is a function of the number of different platforms rather than the number of devices.

$$\text{Diversity} = 1 \text{ to } 2 \text{ methods / platform}$$

If possible, the Attacker should deploy an access method per platform. This means one for Windows, one for Mac, one for Linux, one for Cisco routers, and so forth. It's unlikely that unwitting Defender changes will wipe them all out at once.

This may not be enough in a homongenous network, for example, all Windows computers and Huawei routers. For this, a completely independent backup method must be used. Ideally the primary and backup methods are on different machines, and preferably different segments of the network.

Finally, a third method must be kept on the shelf in reserve. This minimizes the amount deployed while allowing for the rapid repair of an issue.

This three-level strategy is similar in concept to computer backups. There is the primary storage used daily. There is the first backup that can be accessed quickly in case the primary fails, like an external USB hard drive or RAID array. And finally, a second backup is kept offsite in case of theft, fire, or other local disasters.

For a typical corporate network, the Attacker may use a primary implant that communicates over the web, a working backup that uses e-mail, and a third DNS-based one on the shelf should one of the other two stop working one day. (DNS is the last choice for technical reasons including low bandwidth and unreliability.)

Of course, this does not work for every scenario. Sometimes, there really is only one right way of doing something. A well locked down network may have only a single exit point and protocol, but that is the exception.

The best precaution strategy will depend on the Attacker's levels of awareness. The more aware the Attacker can be, the less redundancy and diversity required. If you can see and react to changes quickly, you do not need as many fail-safes. Either way, the Attacker must defend against the little things: a change in server address, the unintended consequences of regular network maintenance, or a hard drive failing, to maintain long-term operational success.

Principle 5: Operational Security

Operational security is the minimization of adversarial exposure, recognition, and reaction to the existence of an operation. It is defensive in nature, though it furthers an offensive mission. Avoiding detection and recognition requires limiting the deployment of technologies and methods without preventing the successful continuation of an operation.

To appreciate operational security, it is useful to understand the concept of relative superiority. In his study of special operations missions, now Admiral William McRaven described *relative superiority* as having superior numbers, firepower, maneuverability, and so on at the point of engagement, even while outnumbered, outgunned, or hemmed in at the macro level.[3]

In essence, relative superiority is operating successfully while literally surrounded by the enemy. McRaven identifies maintaining it as the essential predictor of special operations success.

A similar concept is applicable to CNE. A target network is a hostile environment, one entirely controlled by the "enemy." Relative superiority is gained at the moment of initial access, while the Defender is unaware of the Attacker's presence. At this moment, Attackers have time to cover their tracks, time to solidify their position, time to start surveying, and time to move.

Relative superiority is lost upon discovery. When an attack is recognized, the advantage instantly shifts. The Defender can quarantine what they find and start searching their entire network (often in one swoop) for similar footprints. The Defender now has time to hunt them down, time to reverse engineer anything they find, and time to trace connections.

Operational security is best defined as all that is done before and during an operation that prevents the loss of relative superiority, everything that prevents discovery. It is using signed software like Stuxnet does. It is piggy-backing on a Windows update server to spread like the Flame malware does.

Operational security is the twin of the principle of precaution. Whereas precaution contemplates the effects of the Defender's actions on the Attacker, operational security considers the impact of the Attacker on the Defender.

Minimizing Exposure

An essential part of operational security is minimizing your exposure. This is done through the employment of *stealth*: the leveraging of tools, technologies, and methods that are largely hidden from view, or if in view, unlikely to attract attention. You can't shoot what you *don't* see. (Whether or not you *could* see something is irrelevant.)

Stealth is minimizing the Defender's opportunity to observe artifacts of the operation. It may include explicit hiding, such as removing files or network connections from view. The "copy protection" mechanism that Sony released in 2005 hid its own files from viewing in Windows Explorer.

Stealth may also include cleaning up traces after the fact, such as clearing the history of commands executed on a Linux machine.

Minimizing exposure can entail more than active hiding. It also includes being perfectly visible, but in a manner that is unlikely to be observed. This is why there is malware with filenames such as msupdate.exe and netupdsrv .exe that place themselves in directories with thousands of other files.[4] Hiding in plain sight is common.

Reducing exposure also entails operating where people are not looking or where automated detection is lacking. Using a network printer to tunnel into a network is great operational security. As long as it still prints, who is going to examine the integrity of the software? More to the point, how would someone do it even if they wanted to? The defensive tools do not exist.

Of course, the stealthiest technology is the one not used at all. Every file and every network connection not made is one that cannot be detected. Over deployment of tools is just as susceptible to detection as under deployment is to accidental loss of access.

Yet there must be some level of presence, and all aspects cannot be completely kept from view. This brings us to the next key task of operational security.

Minimizing Recognition

Every operation has some level of exposure to observation. But what *can* be observed is not what matters. Attacker actions must *be* observed and recognized for what they are.

All the technical warnings and signs in the world are irrelevant if the Defender does nothing. Operational security therefore must include minimizing Defenders' recognition of what they do observe. Detection is ultimately a human endeavor, which means that some aspects of human perception and cognition can be abused to minimize recognition.

The first such candidate ripe for abuse is *pattern recognition*. Humans are hardwired to recognize patterns. Our brains are overloaded with sensory input every instant. Patterns are one way the brain quickly extracts the salient details necessary for survival from the immense amount of information. People can instantly recognize even complex patterns, like faces, and more important, recognize anomalies in those patterns.

Therefore, one way to avoid being perceived is to ensure that observable artifacts and actions are kept within an expected pattern.

For example, suppose the Attacker's objective is to retrieve the list of U.S. citizens applying for a security clearance, such as the one pilfered in 2014.[5] Further suppose this information is stored in a database where access to it is well controlled and monitored. One approach may be to retrieve the data from a backup server that routinely copies the data. Any access logs will show that backup server as having accessed the main server, just as expected.

The Attacker may then choose to pull the list off the network at night when the organization normally transfers data to an offsite location. Again, this fits within the expected pattern of bandwidth usage and is unlikely to be recognized as troublesome.

Patterns are the Attacker's friend. Unfortunately, not every action can fit nicely into a regular usage pattern. For example, there is no good cover for expanding access from the external website to the internal accounting system. Those two systems should never communicate directly in a well-architected network.

Because there is no possible pattern to exploit, the Attacker may need to abuse the Defender's perception of causation, another human factor. Everyone who has ever used a computer has had a program crash or the computer freeze. Often these issues are magically fixed by rebooting. Large networks have this problem magnified. The website doesn't load, e-mail doesn't work, or the file share is slower than normal. These kinds of problems happen all the time and usually go away by themselves. Sufficient complexity guarantees some level of anomalies.

When these anomalies do occur, people's reactions will vary with the perceived cause. If a user is unable to log in to a server, he will react differently depending on whether he thinks, "I may have forgotten my password" versus "The server is down." The first cause leads to a few retries, whereas the second results in a phone call to the system administrator.

The human brain is always searching for a cause and develops shortcuts to find them. If a friend eats something and immediately gets sick, then it must be the food. People search backward in time from an effect to the first plausible cause. Proximity in time is a shortcut for cause.

Proximity in space is another shortcut. If a child is standing next to a pile of cookie crumbs, the conclusion is obvious. People search around an event in space for the first plausible explanation. It is hard for people to even consider something beyond these ready explanations. Maybe the friend was already sick before she ate the food, or maybe the dog really did grab a cookie off the counter and make the mess, but good luck convincing the observer.

It follows that if the Attacker can spread out anomalous actions in space and time, they may impact Defenders' perception of cause and minimize recognition. For example, you might perform data exfiltration from a different machine than the one used to access the database. This separates the increased database access from the increased network usage in space.

The Attacker may also space compromising different network segments over a period of months. This separates anomalous network interconnections over time thus obscuring that there may be a common cause. Some malware waits minutes or hours to separate the initial infection from the resulting network traffic. This helps avoid both human and automated detection.

In short, the Attacker can minimize recognition by spacing anomalous actions far enough apart in space and time to keep below the human threshold of perceived cause. This allows Attackers to get away with causing some number of oddities without being recognized.

Occasionally though, even after employing stealth and recognition minimization techniques, to paraphrase Han Solo, even the best get boarded and searched. The Attacker must plan for this as well.

Controlling Reaction

The Defender must find, recognize, and react properly to the presence of the Attacker to fully terminate the operation. The long shot of operational security is controlling Defenders' reactions even after they recognize the intruder. At this stage, relative superiority is lost, and the odds of sustaining the operation are greatly diminished. Still, it is not over until the last point of access is gone.

Other means become necessary. The Attacker may consciously leave in place tools, logs, or other decoys to be found that misdirect Defenders into thinking they have rooted out the problem. Meanwhile the stealthiest tools are directed to remain silent for weeks or months while the dust settles.

Even before detection, the Attacker could willingly allow some inconsequential tool to be exposed, drawing the Defender's attention elsewhere while consuming valuable resources. This exact strategy was employed by thieves to steal millions of dollars in bitcoins, a virtual currency. The Attackers executed a high-profile, highly visible denial-of-service attack to draw attention and resources away from their attack elsewhere. [6]

It is high risk, but with sufficient planning, Attackers may allow deliberate detection to lull Defenders into a false sense of security, allowing Defenders to "confirm" their network defenses are sufficient. Attackers could even go so far as to execute a kind of false flag operation, where they use a tool set that implicates someone else to cover their own tracks.

Attackers cannot completely control what Defenders do after they recognize they are compromised, but carefully orchestrated misdirection can definitely influence their reaction.

Measuring Operational Security

Operational security has substantial costs. It takes knowledge, awareness, and time and requires constant innovation. It trades off against the principle of precaution. The most secure footprint on target is as small as possible, whereas the most precautionary one is as large as possible. The formulas outlined in the principle of precaution help strike the right balance.

$$\text{Points of access per segment} = \text{natural\_log(number of devices)}$$

$$\text{Diversity} = 1 \text{ to } 2 \text{ methods / platform}$$

Operational security can work in tandem with or against awareness. You cannot be operationally secure without understanding the Defender's environment; the more awareness you have, the more secure you can be. But the act of acquiring that awareness is less operationally secure.

Finding the right balance is a multidimensional problem that requires an understanding of the Defender, the threat profile, and an objective evaluation of risk. The last of these is perhaps the most important. An objective evaluation considers the true nature of the specific target, the likelihood of finding the Attacker, and the likely course of action if successful. Attacking a defense contractor is not the same as a retailer.

The most successful operational security strategy will leverage the minimal amount of technical and operational tradecraft necessary for the operation.

Principle 6: Program Security

The Attacker always has two objectives: the success of the given operation and maintaining the ability to conduct future operations. It's a careful balance. "Using a capability" is just another way of saying "potentially exposing a capability."

Program security is the principle of containing damage caused during the compromise of an operation. And no matter how good the Attacker is, some operations will get compromised.

You do not want a failure in one operation impacting another. This also includes future operations against the same target. Like operational security, program security is a form of risk management.

CNE tools are often described as weapons; and though they inflict damage of sorts, the physical analogy does not always hold. Witnessing a gun fire does not change the gun's effectiveness. It can be used to kill just the same. If an enemy captures the gun, it can be replaced by producing a new identical gun.

A technical vulnerability and the corresponding software exploit are different. If a Defender witnesses the deployment of that exploit and analyzes it, they can counter it. They can remove the vulnerable software or reconfigure their systems. They can even render it ineffective against other completely unrelated targets by submitting information about the vulnerability to the software vendor who then disseminates an update.

When patched, there is no way to reproduce the exploit like a physical weapon that compensates for its loss. The time and money spent on development is gone. The so-called weapon cannot be rearmed. An exploit that cost $400 thousand dollars to research and develop can disappear overnight with barely a whimper.

Fashioning an offensive strategy that relies on remaining undetected forever is chasing an impossible reality. For a large-enough offensive program, bad luck and other frictions will trump operational security some of the time. Program security contemplates and prepares for the compromising of Attacker tools and operational methods.

To understand the value of program security, you must first examine what the Attacker has to lose.

Attacker Liabilities

What will the Attacker lose when the operation is compromised? A few days of effort? A few years? How do you even know if the operation is compromised? Answer: you don't, or at least you can never be 100 percent certain. Security companies intentionally sit back and watch for as long as possible in an attempt to lure the Attacker into exposing liabilities.

A *liability* is anything that can be used to impede the Attacker's future operations. They can be technical or not. They vary greatly with each operation and to some extent are Attacker controlled. Yet, the true risk involved depends on the Defender's reaction and capabilities.

The minimal Defender reaction is to quarantine the specific threat detected. If one piece of malware is found, it is removed from the system. Then perhaps the rest of the network is searched for identical instances. Then life returns to normal. Many organizations simply do not have the resources to do much more than keep things running. Others do not have the competency to understand that the damage likely goes well beyond the one tool found.

Most Defenders will attempt a *battle damage assessment (BDA)*. A BDA is a short analysis to determine the best, worst, and likely impact of the Attacker's actions. It attempts to answer the "what":

- What systems were compromised?
- What credit cards were exposed?
- What user accounts?
- What intellectual property and what is its value?

A well-resourced adversary goes beyond a BDA to perform a forensic analysis. This is industry terminology for attempting to do a full accounting of all Attacker actions on the network.

A forensic analysis may take several forms but generally includes a systematic analysis of the Attacker-controlled device, an attempt to find the initial method of entry, and a review of any other systems the Attacker may have touched. It is time- and labor-intensive. It attempts to answer the "who" and the "how":

- Who was it? Which nation state, group, or lone actor?
- How did the Attacker gain initial access?
- How did they maintain and expand access?
- How long were they in the network?
- How did they communicate?

The degree of risk to the Attacker under such analysis is variable. Anthem insurance, Dairy Queen, Lockheed Martin, and the FBI all have different motivations and a disparate set of knowledge, skill, and attention. The worst case for the Attacker is a Defender with a lot to lose. They will be sufficiently skilled and motivated or at least funded well enough to hire competent technical support. Banks (in theory) fall into this category.

Contemplating program security is akin to following the old adage of hoping for the best but planning for the worst. The worst case is the full dissection and publishing of Attacker liabilities, and then having this list incorporated into defenses via security products or practices.

Attacker liabilities fall into one or more of the following broad categories:

- **Identity**—Information regarding the identity of the Attacker to include any accomplices or willing intermediaries.

- **Target pollution**—Information that enables the Defender to identify other Attacker operations and potentially notify other targets.

- **Attack infrastructure**—Information regarding the transit points, drop points, or other Attacker-controlled network infrastructure. Note: Attacker *controlled* is more than Attacker owned or Attacker procured. It can just as easily refer to an innocent third party.

- **Technical vulnerabilities**—Software or hardware vulnerabilities leveraged to gain initial access or to expand access.

- **Technical tools**—Software or hardware tools used to conduct operational actions. These include tools used to remotely control the target, to collect data, to clean up, and so on.

- **Operational methodologies**—Attacker techniques used to avoid detection, expand throughout a network, and more. These may be technical, such as a specific sequence of commands, or nontechnical, such as the way e-mail addresses are gathered during targeting.

Of all these categories, identity, or perhaps more accurately, maintaining anonymity, has an indeterminate and practically priceless value. The Defender cannot arrest, file lawsuits against, or apply diplomatic pressure to an unknown assailant. Identity is the difference between knowing about *an* attacker versus *the* Attacker. True anonymity grants plausible deniability and a measure of security against counterattack on almost any level.

The remaining liabilities have a more calculable cost. How many targets are affected? What is the intelligence or economic value of each? How much time and money was invested into gaining access? What attack infrastructure, technical vulnerabilities, or tools are lost? How much did they cost to create? Are there replacements? If not, how much will these cost? What is the level of lost operational capability?

By explicitly categorizing liabilities, the Attacker can more quickly and reliably determine a cost of failure under myriad circumstances. This is crucial as evaluating and compensating for a failure is generally extremely time-sensitive. The Attacker may have only a few days to determine the ramifications of failure and take appropriate actions. This is more easily accomplished under severe pressure when there is an up-front and ongoing understanding of what is at stake.

Program Security Costs

Protecting each liability is important, but like other strategic principals there are trade-offs. In an ideal world, the Attacker would leverage unique vulnerabilities, tools, infrastructure, and methods against each target. There would be no overlap whatsoever. Even the people involved during the attack would be different so as not to have any similarities in style or preference.

As shown in Figure 7.2, complete duplication would guarantee that one target could not impact another. There would be no target pollution. Any discovered vulnerabilities would be single use and therefore have no impact on operational capabilities.

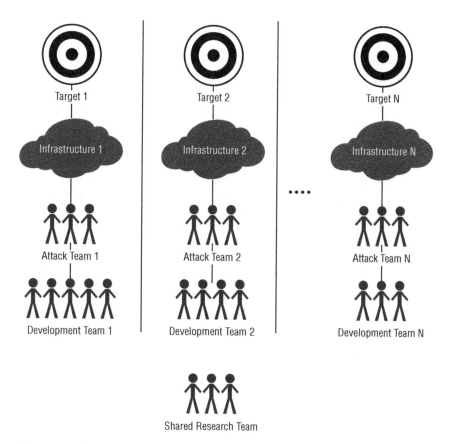

Figure 7.2: Ideal program security

Is this level of redundancy possible? Perhaps for one extremely valuable target. But it simply does not scale beyond that. There are not enough resources.

Instead, the Attacker must calculate and weigh the costs involved in an operational compromise. Costs are not one-sided though. There are both Attacker and Defender costs to consider.

The Attacker costs are in reproducing, replacing, or outright losing a capability. The Defender's costs are in defeating operational and program security: the cost of detection, analysis, mitigation, and finally the cost of distributing the analysis, defense, or mitigation to others.

To establish the priority of resources, the Attacker can think of the associated costs in terms of a simple equation:

$$\text{Attacker Costs} < \text{Defender Costs}$$

Effective program security means keeping this equation valid. Expanded, this equation becomes:

$$
\begin{array}{c}
\begin{array}{c}
\text{Replacement cost} \\
\underline{+\ \text{Loss of capability}} \\
\text{Attacker costs}
\end{array}
\quad < \quad
\begin{array}{c}
\text{Detection cost} \\
\text{Analysis cost} \\
\text{Mitigation cost} \\
\underline{+\ \text{Distribution cost}} \\
\text{Defender costs}
\end{array}
\end{array}
$$

Several consequences become apparent by evaluating each variable's relationship in this expanded equation.

Low-Cost Capabilities

First, consider a capability with a low replacement cost: a simple downloader. A downloader is a program whose sole purpose is to reach out, download, and execute another piece of malware. They are used extensively as the first stage in client-side attacks.

A downloader is low cost, even trivial, to create: a developer could knock one out in a single day. Looking at the equation, you can conclude the Attacker doesn't need to expend much effort to maintain program security for these tools because the Defender's costs of detecting, analyzing, mitigating, and distributing a fix will be higher. This helps explain why there are millions of downloaders.

For low-cost capabilities, the Attacker can preemptively duplicate the capability and use unique versions across targets. That way, there is minimal to no overlap and little risk of target pollution.

Increasing the Cost of Detection

In considering the other variables, assume the Attacker costs are nontrivial. The goal remains to keep the equation tilted in the Attacker's favor.

One way of tipping the equation is to increase the cost of detection. Put another way, Attackers should look to improve their operational security without dramatically increasing their own replacement costs.

There is not a simple relationship between the amount invested and the increase in operational security. For example, removing a single line of code from a program is sometimes enough to render it not flagged by antivirus products. It's a small change with a huge benefit. Other times, a big effort yields minimal improvement. A complete rewrite of a kernel-mode rootkit, a sophisticated attack tool, is worthless if a defensive product triggers on its method of installation.

Recognizing that investment and operational security can be somewhat independent allows the Attacker to focus on value per cost, instead of naively pursuing operational security at any cost. It may be better to create multiple low-cost capabilities that are more easily detected than one super method that, while harder to detect, is expensive to replace.

This is the conclusion much of the criminal industry has reached. How else can we explain the millions of new instances of malware the defensive industry catches each year? Low-cost incremental improvements to stealth keep program security tilted in the Attacker's favor.

The same thinking applies to infrastructure. It may be better to use cheaply acquired but unreliable infrastructure than more durable and high-cost alternatives.

A hybrid strategy may yield the best results. Leverage low-cost detectable techniques and methods for day-to-day operations while leaving in place high-cost-to-replace and high-cost-to-detect methods as a contingency. This "give them something to find" strategy is a hedge. It allows Attackers to keep the program security equation in their favor while minimizing cost.

Increasing the Cost of Analysis

Another approach to tilting the program security equation in the Attacker's favor is to increase the cost of analysis. If something is difficult to analyze, it is difficult to counter. There are three main ways of increasing the cost of analysis.

Antireverse Engineering

Antireverse engineering techniques make it more difficult to statically analyze a technical capability. *Static analysis* is when you look at a particular piece of technology (software source code, machine code, or hardware circuit board layouts) and attempt to determine what exactly that technology does and how. It is like taking apart a car while it is off, examining all the parts and their relationships to each other, and using that information to determine how the car works and what it does.

A simple example of an antireverse engineering technique is a program that requires the user to enter a password before it decrypts and runs its main functionality. The main portion of the program cannot be analyzed unless the person knows that password. Another technique may attempt to hide or obfuscate calls into the operating system by invoking them in nonstandard ways. This hinders the analyst's ability to determine what the program does.

There's nothing inherently "bad" about antireverse engineering. Yes, Attackers use it to hinder analysis. But game makers employ these techniques to keep people from hacking their games. Software companies use it to stop people from unlawfully copying their software. Security products use it to help prevent Attackers from breaching them. Antireverse engineering techniques have dual use.

Antidebugging

Antidebugging techniques make it more difficult to dynamically analyze a technical capability. *Dynamic analysis* is analyzing a technology while it is running, often under controlled scenarios. Extending the car analogy, the analyst can start and drive the car. He can stomp on the gas pedal, hit the brakes, or shift gears and see what that does. He can even replace the entire transmission with one he already understands and see how that impacts the car. Dynamic analysis scrutinizes a system while in use.

There are several techniques to make dynamic analysis more difficult. One common antidebugging method (and the namesake of the technique) is to prevent someone from attaching a debugger, a program that enables an analyst to step through the software one instruction at a time. This may be done through any number of techniques including manipulating privileges or creating dependencies on timing.

Another common method in malicious software is to attempt to detect when someone is analyzing the program. For example, the software may try to detect whether it is running inside a virtual machine, a type of controlled environment for analyzing software. If so, then it exits, or perhaps if the malware is clever, it does something else innocuous.

Of course, there are anti-antidebuggers an analyst may use to detect this behavior and modify the environment to fool the software. It boils down to an arms race, but one that is generally won by the analyst.

Like antireverse engineering, there are legitimate (okay questionably legitimate) uses for antidebugging such as Digital Rights Management software that attempts to block copying protected content. As such, there are commercial antidebugging tools that address the need.

Capability Diffusion

Capability diffusion is the act of splitting capabilities into smaller components that are difficult to link together. For example, the capability of retrieving data from a database could be broken up as follows:

- Program 1—The data collector queries the database and stores the results to a file server.
- Program 2—The data mover breaks the file into small chunks and e-mails copies to an internal account.
- Program 3—The data exfiltrator intercepts the e-mails and redirects them to the Attacker.

These three programs can run on three different machines, with different accounts, on different schedules as shown in Figure 7.3.

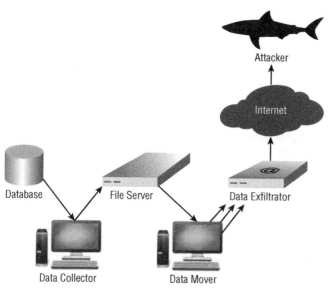

Figure 7.3: Example capability diffusion

The diffusion provides a level of security. If people find Program 2, the data mover, they will see e-mails sent that apparently never arrive. There is no indication of how the data gets to the file server in the first place or where it ends up. There is no obvious link to Programs 1 or 3. Though removing Program 2 may interrupt the operation, unless the other two programs are found, the Attacker has minimized their losses. The same argument applies if either Program 1 or 3 is found first.

The preceding example is simple. In reality, capabilities can be broken into a dozen pieces spread through a single machine or across a network. Capability diffusion can vastly increase the time and expertise necessary to find all traces of the Attacker.

Disadvantages of Increasing the Analysis Cost

Each of the three methods of antireverse engineering, antidebugging, and capability diffusion increase the Defender's analysis costs. And depending on how hard they are to implement, these methods may or may not substantially increase the Attacker's replacement costs.

Yet, despite the clear benefits, it's not necessarily always in the Attacker's best interest to make things difficult to analyze. Even if Defenders have difficulty determining what something does, they may still broadly classify it as "bad."

More to the point, difficulty of analysis is an indication that something *is* bad. The antianalysis techniques could form a signature of sorts that could be more easily detected. And remember, getting detected is equivalent to losing relative superiority, the first step in having every aspect of the operation wrapped up. Carelessly increasing the cost of analysis may actually lower the Defender's total costs and decrease program security.

Also, no sound strategy can rely solely on an adversary's inability to analyze an attack. The attack on Iranian centrifuges known as Stuxnet proves this point. It was without question the most sophisticated malware publicly known at the time of its discovery. Yet, although it took months to reverse engineer its capabilities and purpose, it was done nonetheless. It just took time and money, and not even the target's money as the security community did the analysis for free.

Increasing analysis cost is a worthy goal, but it must be done without increasing the Attacker's technology replacement costs or lowering the Defender's detection costs.

Increasing the Cost of Mitigation and Distribution

Finally, the Attacker should strive to increase the Defender's costs of mitigation and distribution. *Mitigation* is the cost of preventing the Attacker's actions in the first place, or cleaning up the mess after an attack is successfully detected. *Distribution* is the cost associated with either acquiring that knowledge or sharing it with others.

Antivirus signatures are the most common method of mitigation. After the Attacker is caught once and a software tool is submitted to an antivirus company, signatures are developed that "catch" the Attacker tool and remove it from everywhere the antivirus product is installed.

The cost of mitigation in this case is the cost of purchasing, installing, and maintaining the product. The cost of distribution is minimal.

Without a signature, system administrators incur the costs of manually removing malicious software themselves. This can range from trivial to almost impossible, especially when not all components are known. (The U.S. State Department spent over 3 months in early 2015 attempting to remove a known infiltration of their e-mail systems.[7])

Other mitigations operate at the network level. These include whitelisting or blacklisting certain network addresses or blocking certain protocols. These mitigations attempt to block the Attacker's ability to communicate. Most Attacker software is rendered useless without the ability to communicate.

Network mitigation costs are in purchasing and maintaining the requisite technology. These products can range from thousands to tens of thousands of dollars and often require a highly technical staff to maintain.

The distribution costs of sharing network mitigation information are also higher. They require human action. If one company blocks a specific network address as malicious, this information is not automatically posted. And if and when it is communicated, it takes time for other companies to make changes to their networks. And each network will be set up differently, so simple step-by-step instructions will not apply.

This model of distribution is, of course, an oversimplification. High-level ISPs and government-level Computer Emergency Response Teams (CERTs) communicate threats with each other, and those cover a substantial portion of the Internet. New network products are also incorporating the ability to automatically communicate issues between different companies. Regardless, it remains far more costly to communicate network-level mitigations effectively.

Defenders' mitigation costs are real, but the trend is in their favor. Security products are getting cheaper and providing more value. Part of that value is finding more effective ways of distributing that information to their customers, which works against the Attacker.

One Attacker "solution" would be to collude with security companies. In fact, some fear that whether through direct pressure or a security company's sense of patriotism, this is already happening.[8] China even went so far as to bar U.S.-based Symantec and Russian-based Kaspersky from its procurement.[9] But even if governments and companies were in league, it does not solve the Attacker's problems. Security companies are based in the United States, Russia, China, Israel, Czech Republic, Germany, Spain, the Netherlands, and more. No single entity is going to get the cooperation of all of them.

So how can an Attacker respond? Directly increasing the cost of distribution is a losing proposition. The incentives to share information will increase as organizations such as the SEC impose notification requirements. Meanwhile the disincentives are decreasing as the stigma associated with getting hacked disappears.

In an old Western, if a bank robber's picture is put up at the post office, what are his options? He could move to another state and exploit the lack of communication. But that tactic is increasingly difficult. What then? He can change his appearance. He can find an accomplice. He can rob places at night when no one is there. He can change his modus operandi and go after restaurants instead of banks. (Okay, maybe that's just *Pulp Fiction*).

What do all these tactics have in common? A simple strategy. Decrease the value of any information shared. This does not increase the mitigation cost per se, but it decreases its effectiveness.

Attackers can decrease the value of a signature by employing metamorphic techniques or by rotating network addresses, that is, by changing their appearance. They can decrease the value of detection heuristics by acting more and more like a regular user or in ways that another target may consider acceptable. The options are endless.

As mitigation and distribution costs decrease, the only option is to decrease their value. There may be more communication, but the Attacker can make it increasingly useless. (Come to think of it, this is a reasonable description of the Internet.)

A stolen credit card is worth about $1 on the black market. What is the cost to the Attacker of a signature or other mitigation? Answer: the development and deployment costs of circumventing that mitigation. By leveraging a variety of techniques, the Attacker can push down that value and help keep the equation of program security in their favor.

Measuring Program Security

Program security underlies all other strategic principles. The other principles are of little consequence if the Attacker loses the ability to operate or if all operations are wrapped up when any one of them is. Unfortunately, the benefits of program security are recognized only intermittently, whereas the costs are immediate.

Emphasizing program security runs contrary to three common human failings: prioritizing the immediate over the long term, overconfidence in one's abilities or fortunes, and the underestimation of adversarial abilities or adverse conditions. This is a dangerous mix.

People overemphasize the present and discount the future, especially when the future is uncertain. Take climate change. We can argue about the severity of the impact climate change will have on the world. Yet, no one is going to argue that building another 300 coal-fired power plants in China is good for humanity's long-term health and well-being. Still, they will be built because China values the immediate increase in the standard of living while discounting the long-term environmental costs. We make decisions like this all the time, whether in saving for retirement or choosing to eat just one more slice of pizza. Short-term decisions are the norm.

People also fall prey to overconfidence. Whether it's the "too good to get caught" hacker or the philandering politician, hubris is an all too common downfall. Breaking into systems is almost too easy. Attackers start to attribute their continual success to skill, rather than the more apt analogy that they are playing chess against a 12 year old. The weak state of defensive security breeds an arrogance that is proven right time and again, until it fails catastrophically.

And when that failure happens, as it will, Attackers will be more prone to blame it on bad luck than on capable Defenders. Experience teaches that Defenders are ineffective, so it's hard to imagine that it's actually Bobby Fischer sitting across the table and you never stood a chance. Easy wins make it difficult to imagine losing.

Given these human traits of short-term thinking, overconfidence, and underestimation, maintaining program security will always be a tough sell. It is not nearly as exciting as new capabilities. It often provides no immediate benefit, no new access, and no new operational prowess.

Actually, program security provides no benefit whatsoever until an operation is compromised. By definition, it entails developing redundant capabilities. Together, this makes program security ripe for "cost savings." Yet it is essential to maintaining sustained access across multiple targets. Without program security, the ability to conduct operations will crumble.

Of course, there is a balance that must be found. Creating redundant capabilities for everything is cost prohibitive. Every capability is not essential.

To fashion that balance, the Attacker must measure the costs of losing a capability against the Defender's costs of detecting, analyzing, mitigating, and distributing the mitigation. This, in turn, requires knowing where and how every capability is deployed and how its loss may impact other existing and potential future operations.

In short, program security requires meticulous record keeping, constant reevaluation of risk, and the proactive development of contingencies. Sound familiar? It's basically the same thing that every modern competitive business requires. Achieving this level of data-oriented decision making is what separates professional Attackers from the amateurs.

Crafting an Offensive Strategy

Do not try and bend the spoon. That's impossible. Instead, only try to realize the truth. . . There is no spoon. . . Then you'll see, that it is not the spoon that bends, it is only yourself.

—**The Matrix**

Crafting an offensive strategy requires asking the right questions. It is cliché, but the most important questions look inward first. You must first answer the high-level questions about the nature of the offensive operations and the organization that will implement the strategy. These include the following:

- What are the political, economic, military, or other goals of the set of operations?
- What if any legal limitations are there?
- What are the political, diplomatic, and military implications of success?
  - Of partial success?
  - Of silent failure?
  - Of exposed failure?
- What level of risk is acceptable?

- How does this set of operations complement other instruments of national power?

- How does it detract?

- What are the resources you are willing to bring to bear on the goal?

- How is the organization funded?

- How is that funding prioritized?

- Is long-term funding available, and if so, how is it appropriated versus short-term funding?

- How are efforts and technological developments evaluated, ranked, and when necessary killed?

- What are the limitations on reshaping the organization to meet operational needs?

- How is leadership selected and developed?

- How is the necessary operational and technical talent recruited, trained, and retained?

Answers to these questions will vary greatly between country, agency, or individual attack teams. Candidness is a must. Computer operations are not magic. It's easy to say you are going to "hire 5,000 cyber warriors," as the U.S. Cyber Command stated in 2013. It's a much harder problem to determine where these people will come from, what their pay will be, and the potential career progression. The best strategy in the world is irrelevant if it is poorly funded and administered.

Sections of bookstores are devoted to what it takes to create and lead a successful organization, so let's simply assume that there is a well-funded and well-organized entity and that the previous high-level questions have been sufficiently addressed. What then?

It is time to consider the more technical aspects of an offensive strategy. Starting with the level of available resources and the ideal operational objectives, you can develop and evaluate an attack strategy using the strategic principles as guidance. A sample set of questions might include the following.

Knowledge

- Will the strategy focus on the technical or the psychological?

- What up-front expertise is required? What can be learned as needed?

- What can be learned through scholarship versus what requires experience?

- What are the top "X" technologies that will be encountered?

- What is the proper balance between new and old technologies?

- What knowledge must be kept internal?

Awareness

- What is the reaction time of the offensive organization to events?
- What does the reaction time need to be to make awareness effective?
- What is most critical to be aware of?
- How do you monitor those things?
- Can the monitoring be automated or does it require people?
- What is the impact on operational security?

Innovation

- What assumptions does the defensive market make? How can these be exploited?
- What part of the operational life cycle is the Attacker weakest in?
- What innovation must be funded internally?
- What can be shared?
- What can be leveraged from the hacker and academic communities? Where are these communities most likely to innovate?
- What areas have the most applicability for the least investment?

Precaution

- Given the tools in use, what unwitting actions could the Defender take that would disrupt the operation?
- Or what combination of actions?
- Will the Attacker have any advanced notice?
- Will the Attacker be aware when these actions occur? What is the lead time for becoming aware?
- What is the likelihood of each action?
- What is the cost of mitigating each action?
- What is the lead time necessary for mitigating it on the fly? How does this compare to the level of awareness?

Operational Security

- What is the defensive capability and expertise of the set of targets?
- What is the weakest link in operational security for each operation?
- For each capability, what is the balance between true stealth and hiding among the noise; that is, to avoid being seen verses to avoid being recognized? What is the cost difference in creating these capabilities?

- What decreases in operational security can be tolerated for improvements in precaution?
- What is the expected reaction of a given target? How can that reaction be managed?

Program Security

- What is the value of a given operation versus the value of the tools used?
- How do you increase the cost of detection across a broad range of capabilities while gaining the economy of scale that keeps corresponding development costs down?

Knowledge

- How do you verify that a tool is "clean" and will withstand analysis? What level of analysis?
- What is the current state of defensive technology and its ability to predict unseen Attacker tools from known ones?
- What is the balance between code and technology reuse and development cost?

This is a partial list. A full list of questions can be created only by applying the strategic principles to the specific Attacker. One Attacker may "throw money" at program security by creating duplicate capabilities. Another may devalue the benefits of awareness as they only target low-security entities that are easily repenetrated. It all depends.

Regardless of Attackers' resources and their objectives, the strategic principles provide a framework for crafting a coherent tailored offensive strategy. Of course, any strategy will be iterative. And it will require re-evaluation every 4 months or so. But framing your thoughts to ask the right questions makes this task easier and much more likely to be successful.

Modular Frameworks

What do Stuxnet, Flame, Red October, Zeus, the ZeroAccess rootkit, and more have in common? It's not country of origin, communication methods, or intended targets. Answer: they all have a plug-in-based architecture. These are not just attack tools, they are attack platforms.

Plug-ins are pieces of software that extend the functionality of an existing program. Oracle Java, Adobe Flash, Microsoft Windows Media Player, and Apple QuickTime are all common examples of plug-ins that give added functionality to a web browser. Though browser plug-ins are the most common, many other popular software programs support extension via plug-ins. Photoshop, WordPress, and CorelDRAW can be similarly extended.

Well, a plug-in architecture is not just for legitimate software providers anymore. Modern offensive tool kits are composed of different components that can be fitted together like Legos® to form the whole. Specific features, or modules, are separated and mixed and matched statically or dynamically as needed.

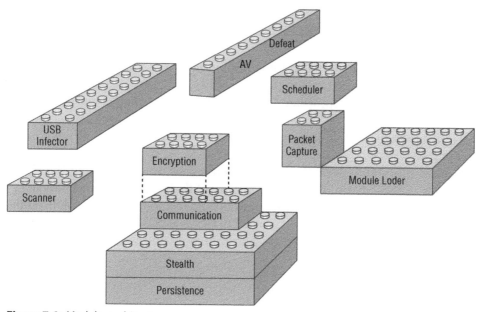

Figure 7.4: Modular architecture

Why are they designed this way? The advantages of a modular architecture are clear if you consider the offensive principles.

It allows more economic use of resources. With a defined interface between components, different parts can be farmed out to different groups for simultaneous development. Specialized teams can focus on one aspect of functionality, be it communication, collection, or privilege escalation without worrying about how other parts work. A modular approach decreases the amount of knowledge required per developer.

Further, this approach allows portions of tools to be hot swappable. For example, a single beaconing backdoor could be retrofitted with a different method of communication. This increases network level diversity without having to reinvent the core functionality of the tool.

Modules also vastly improve operational security. With a dynamic loading capability, functional components can be pulled down and loaded directly into memory, leaving nothing to find on disk. It raises forensic analysis to a whole new level of difficulty. By it's very nature, modularity makes capability diffusion the standard.

Modules enable the ability to replace parts of tools, thereby lowering the replacement cost should only a single component get detected. This increases program security.

In short, Stuxnet and the other platforms look like they were designed by committee because the ensuing modularity provides an all-around strategic advantage.

A Note on Tactical Decisions

Strategic principles do not need to be limited to crafting strategy. Leveraging these principles can also improve tactical decisions.

(Note: the most important step is to actually make tactical decisions. While this is obvious in the early stages of the operational life cycle, it is easy to fall into a pattern of inattentiveness, passivity, and indecision with sustained access.)

Determining the best tactical move often comes down to asking the right questions. Attackers can improve the quality of their questions, and thus their tactical decisions, by examining the situation and fashioning questions through the lens of the framework.

For example, consider the tactical question: how and when should data be exfiltrated out of this network?

A sample set of questions might be

Humanity

- Does this transfer fit in with normal daytime/nighttime routines?
- Will the transfer cause a slowdown in the network?
- If so, who would notice? What is their likely reaction?

Economy

- Does the organization have the capacity to monitor bandwidth?
- If so, are the administrators too busy to check said bandwidth logs?
- Do they have the technical expertise in-house to investigate if anything is found?

Access

- What protocols are allowed out of this network?
- Which users and devices on the network regularly have outside access?

Knowledge

- What devices exist that monitor bandwidth?
- What are their default thresholds?

Awareness

- Are there network-monitoring tools in place?
- Are bandwidth quotas enforced?
- Are there limitations on the timing of access?
- Where should the Attacker expand to determine this?

Innovation

- Can data be exfiltrated over a nonmonitored protocol?
- If not, what would it take to develop this?

Precaution

- What is the backup exfiltration method if this one is cut off?

Operational Security

- What are the risks in expanding access to ascertain network monitoring posture?
- Can the points of access be separated such that if data exfiltration is detected, command and control will not be compromised?

Program Security

- Where else has this exfiltration method been used?
- What pattern or signature could be created if detected?

Answer the questions on this list, and the answer to whether exfiltrating should occur during the day or night will be obvious. Evaluating a tactical question within the framework leads to smarter tactical decisions while avoiding undermining the strategic considerations.

Summary

Developing strategy is a daunting task. The enormous breadth, depth, and continual motion of technology can be overwhelming.

The question then becomes what framework can organize your thinking to cut through the chaos. What framework will allow you to develop and evaluate the efficacy of a strategy? One starts by recognizing some truths that emerge from careful consideration:

- There are a few bedrock principles: the humanity of the space, the economy of resources, and the unstoppable possibility of access.

- The goal of CNE can be simplified. Most operations require sustained, undetected access. And those that do not will often be improved by it.

- Each side has certain frictions.

- Each side has certain asymmetric advantages and disadvantages.

From this foundation, you can derive offensive principles for preparing for operations. The common elements to all operations are knowledge, awareness, innovation, precaution, operational security, and program security. Together these principles create a framework for evaluating any offensive strategy.

In the next chapter, we'll explore defensive strategy and how it must counter these principles.

Defensive Strategy

In trying to defend everything, he defended nothing.
—Frederick the Great

Corporate security is losing the battle. It is not from lack of technical expertise. Nor is it a lack of research, malware analysis, or cases to study. It is not from the absence of known good defensive practices. It is not from a lack of money. J.P. Morgan, ExxonMobil, and Rolls-Royce have all been compromised, and these companies are not exactly known for just scraping by.

The central reason for continual defeat is the widespread lack of acknowledgment that the Attacker has a strategy.

The Empire Strikes Back comes to mind:

Luke: I don't believe it.

Yoda: That is why you fail.

This oversight manifests in the continued acceptance, deployment, and redeployment of inherently insecure technologies. It shines through as defensive tactics remain static and on balance, failures.

Attackers are not mindless. There is a strategy and a purpose behind their actions. Defensive tactics fail because they do not account for the existence of this strategy.

Failed Tactics

Search for **top 10 security tips** on the web, and practically every result will include running antivirus software or will have advice on password choice. Other suggestions will include avoiding opening attachments, browsing shady websites, or installing untrusted software. This latter list can be summed up as "training users not to do bad security things."

These tips are solid suggestions. Yet they do not change the dynamics of the conflict. To see why, you must examine each tactic in light of the proceeding chapters.

Antivirus and Signature-Based Detection

Signature-based detection is meant to be preventive. It works by looking for a specific set of code or data. Companies that provide signature-based detection analyze malicious software (generally an automated process) and create a massive list of "known bad" indicators that is pushed to their security products. The products then compare every file, Registry key, and every running program against that list and quarantine anything that matches. Security products also use heuristic signatures, which is the industry way of saying it monitors for certain types of "bad" behavior.

There are several ways the Attacker can avoid these products. First, and most obvious, is don't be on the bad list. If the Attacker's software is never seen by the antivirus companies, then there will be no code signature, and it will not be caught.

Second, the Attacker can avoid executing bad behavior. The trick is determining what constitutes bad, but this can be determined through trial and error or reverse engineering.

Third, the Attacker can avoid being seen by the program. There are many stealth techniques that an Attacker can use to avoid getting scanned.

In 2005, Sony, in a monumental failure of judgment, software development, and marketing, decided to protect its music by surreptitiously installing a program that blocked a user's ability to copy music CDs on Windows. To stop its copy protection software from getting uninstalled, Sony hid all files, processes, and Registry entries that began with the name sys. Put aside that malware instantly started piggybacking on top of this feature by calling itself a variation of sys. The real question is if Sony can write software to do this, why can't anyone else? The answer is the Attacker can and does. Though antivirus has improved, Attackers continue to find ways to avoid getting scanned.

There are many more ways to render antivirus ineffective; the larger point is antivirus does not do so well against well-funded Attackers. Even the purveyors of antivirus software recognize its limitations.

Turning on only the signature-based anti-virus components of endpoint solutions alone are not enough in a world that is changing daily from attacks and threats.[1]
—Symantec regarding *The New York Times* intrusion

The truth is, consumer-grade antivirus products can't protect against targeted malware created by well-resourced nation states…targeted attacks like these go to great lengths to avoid antivirus products on purpose.[2]
—Mikko Hypponen: Chief Research Officer of F-Secure regarding the Stuxnet attack

So everyone agrees that antivirus is not cutting it anymore. But why? Antivirus companies have billions of dollars and thousands of smart technical employees. So it isn't resources.

Traditional antivirus is doomed to fail because it does not impact any asymmetry. Most products are less than $100 and readily available. Therefore, the Attacker's advantage in analysis is unaltered. The Attacker can simply purchase the product, tear it apart, and find weaknesses.

The Attackers' advantage in developing custom software remains an asset. They can test their software against the antivirus repeatedly, modifying it as needed to circumvent being detected. Some have even gone so far as to automate this process and offer it as a gray market service to other Attackers.

Traditional antivirus is further doomed because it does not introduce much in the way of frictions. Again, everything about the product is knowable before the operation. A sudden release of a code signature is possible, though the chicken-and-egg problem remains. The antivirus company must have already detected the product to develop the signature.

A heuristic update could certainly introduce variability, but this goes against the antivirus companies' business model. Most companies introduce major heuristic feature updates once a year, with the release of the next version of the product as a way to induce updates. When released, this creates a race between how fast the Attacker can adapt to the new version versus how fast the Defender upgrades. Given the general pace of corporate upgrades, my money is on the Attacker.

Finally, signature-based antivirus fails—and will continue to fail—because it does not counter any strategic principle. The acquisition of knowledge about the product has a fixed cost.

Awareness of what product the target is running also has a fixed cost. It is trivial to determine the brand and exact version of the product via a rudimentary survey if the Attacker has access to any computer on the Defender's network.

Even without any kind of access, this information can often be found just by searching the web. Many security companies offer testimonials and press releases announcing new customers as part of their marketing. Symantec has a list of more than 300 customer success stories. It's a safe bet these entities run

Symantec products. A search of job postings and support forums may also work. Even a helpful write-up of a previous intrusion may reveal which brand of products are installed.

Should all this fail, it may be possible to just call up random employees and ask what antivirus their company uses by conducting a fake market survey or by attempting to sell them a different product.

This kind of security product awareness is low cost to acquire and low cost to maintain. A wholesale change of antivirus software running across a corporate network is a nontrivial task and is unlikely to happen. In short, the Attacker barely needs to get out of bed to gain and keep awareness of what antivirus products the target is running.

Circumventing antivirus products does require innovation. But as mentioned before, products historically have substantially updated only once a year, hardly a breakneck pace to keep up with. Precaution and operational security are affected, but again, only in entirely predictable ways.

The only saving grace of antivirus products is an increase to the cost of program security. Attackers have to factor in that if they are caught in one place and a signature is created, it can affect other operations.

This is the only reason to run antivirus products and why it should still be used. It eliminates the low hanging fruit, the deployment of tools that have already been caught by other means or by their relationship to existing malware. But eliminating the low hanging fruit, while useful, does not in any way alter the strategic dynamics.

Password Policies

There are two common password policies that are widely suggested. Both policies have failed to stem the tide of intrusions.

The first policy is to choose a strong password. Most everyone has tried signing up for an account where the site requires a minimum password length or some combination of uppercase and lowercase characters, numbers, or punctuation. This is because the strength of the password is defined as how long it would take a computer to guess it assuming it was chosen at random.

The longer the password, the better. The more types of characters used, the better. A six-character password that is chosen from the 26 lowercase letters at random yields 300 million different possible combinations. This sounds like a lot, but at a million attempts per second, it takes only 5 minutes to try every possibility. An eight-character password chosen from the 52 uppercase and lowercase letters plus 10 numbers and 13 different symbols yields 1 quadrillion (10^{15}) possibilities. At a million attempts per second, it will take around 30 years to try all possibilities.

So it's clear that an eight-character password chosen at random is secure enough. And each additional character in the latter example makes it 75 times harder to break. So what's the problem?

As it turns out, people are terrible at choosing random passwords. Even when there are technical constraints that force users to pick different characters, the intent of these constraints is often circumvented through using passwords such as Password123. In fact, according to an analysis of 6.5 million leaked passwords by Mark Burnett, an astounding 91 percent of the password choices were contained in a list of only 1,000 unique passwords.[3] A similar analysis of leaked 4-digit pins found that a mere 61 unique pins (out of 9,999 possible) could be used to compromise a third of all users.[4]

These examples do come from biased samples: the dataset is only from sources that were hacked; the password policies are at best nonuniform and at worst nonexistent; and so on. Yet the point is clear; any large-enough group of people is just not that original. Truly random passwords are too hard to create and remember.

The second policy is to avoid reusing passwords among different systems. This prevents the Attacker from leveraging a password from one system to gain access to another. As shown in Figure 8.1, this is how the company HBGary was hacked in 2011. A low-security system was broken into; the passwords were stolen and cracked; and those passwords were then used to access a more sensitive system.[5]

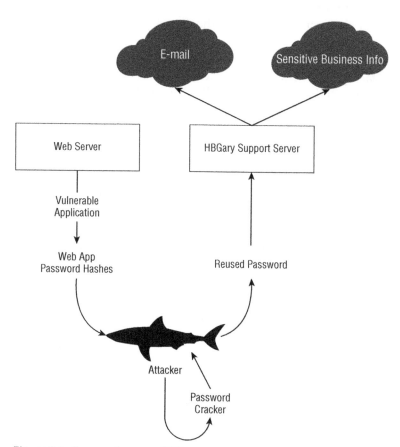

Figure 8.1: Password reuse at HBGary

Avoiding reusing passwords is a great idea…in theory. The problem is there is no way to enforce this policy within an organization—never mind across different organizations. A typical user may have passwords on Amazon.com, Facebook, Gmail, Pinterest, Twitter, Snapchat, a bank login, a company login, an ATM pin, a voice mail access, a garage door code, not to mention every commercial website that requires one to create an account to view or buy something or another. It's too much to keep straight.

It's a nice idea to say that each site should have a different login. But because there's no way to enforce this, there's a good chance that hacking an employee's LinkedIn account is going to yield company login passwords for some percentage of users.

Both requiring strong passwords and avoiding password reuse run counter to human memory and ability. They ignore the foundational principle of humanity.

But suppose passwords did not involve people, that an organization employed only robots who followed policy. Or more realistically, suppose everyone installed and used a password manager, a program that eases the recall and use of long randomized passwords. Further suppose the password manager had no security vulnerabilities itself, a doubtful proposition.

How does a perfect password policy affect the Attacker's strategy? In short, it doesn't.

It may make gaining initial access harder, though by now few organizations will have outward-facing infrastructure with weak passwords. It may also slow down access expansion. Yet the Attacker can still accomplish both of these tasks through a variety of vulnerabilities, password capture tools, or other methods of piggybacking on legitimate access. Strong passwords may require a few new tactics, but the strategy is the same.

After initial access is achieved, strong passwords have little impact on the Attacker's economy of resources. No new knowledge is needed. Awareness is the same. New innovation may be needed, but nothing beyond what the Attacker is already doing. The Attacker is already in a constant cycle of replenishing an arsenal of vulnerabilities through research, development, and purchases. Strong passwords impose no additional burden on precaution, operational security, or program security.

Like antivirus products, it is not that strong passwords are bad. They are very important on an individual level to secure online logins. It's just that alone, even if perfectly implemented, they will not change much of anything when it comes to espionage.

User Training

The theory behind user training is that you can get users to stop doing "stupid" things that cause insecurity. This is a great theory, but curiosity continues to kill the cat when there is a picture of Anna Kournikova attached.

User training has not measurably improved things in the decade since hundreds of thousands of people infected themselves by attempting to view images of the aforementioned tennis star. People still open attachments if they fit what they expect to receive. Users still follow links they find interesting.

Even RSA, the well-known security company and maker of two-factor authentication tokens, was undone by an enticing e-mail with an attachment:

> *The e-mails were sent to what Rivner said was a small group of RSA employees, at least one of whom pulled the message out of a spam folder, opened it, and then opened the malicious attachment.*[6]

—Dennis Fisher, threatpost.com

Note that the automated detection system *worked* exactly as intended. The e-mail was moved to a spam folder, which implicitly marked it as suspicious. And yet, a user at a computer security company still opened it.

User training fails because it does not alter any asymmetry or induce any new friction. It ignores that people are curious and form habits, manifestations of humanity and economy, respectively. Leveraging psychological knowledge and specific target awareness, the Attacker can often induce user behavior in spite of any training.

Perhaps there is some form of training that will work, but a once-a-year class with no follow-up incentives or punishments will not overcome natural tendencies. Until such time as there are real positive and negative consequences to user mistakes, user training will remain a box to be checked with little discernible effect.

Again, organizations should attempt to curb user ignorance just as they should run antivirus software and enforce strong passwords. All three of these tactics may help weed out less sophisticated attacks. But as Sun Tzu advised long ago, "Attack the enemy's strategy." All three examples fail to do this, and that is why they fail.

Crafting a Defensive Strategy

How does an organization counter the Attacker? Ideally, there would be a national strategy that incorporates government and business acting in concert. However, there are valid legal, business, civil liberty, not to mention technical and security concerns that make such a grand strategy impractical for the foreseeable future. If and until these obstacles are worked through, what plan of strategy should an individual Defender follow?

Step 1 is to avoid recreating the wheel. Start with one of the several existing guides for defense. The SANS Institute puts out *Twenty Critical Security Controls for Effective Cyber Defense.*[7] The U.S. National Security Agency offers the *Manageable Network Plan*[8] as well as a variety of individual security configuration guides.

Many guides offer solutions that factor in economy, the up-front and reoccurring costs, humanity, the difficulty of implementation, and user resistance.

Each guide also encourages tailoring its advice to the specific organization to be most effective. So the question really becomes not what could be done, but how to take the voluminous amount of defensive information and tailor it appropriately. Attacks are tailored. The defense must be as well.

Tailoring begins with Step 2, following the cliché, "Know thyself." What is most valuable? Business plans? Credit card numbers? Manufacturing controls? Drone pilot control systems? Crafting a strategy requires understanding the goals of the organization and what is truly essential to support those goals. Keep in mind that saying "Everything is important" is the same as saying "Nothing is important."

Step 3 is to develop a data classification system. This is applying a risk management mentality to what is deemed important. On a personal level, risk management is intuitive. A safe-deposit box is high security but low convenience. So people put in jewelry, birth certificates, or anything that is difficult to replace and need not be readily accessible. However, people leave tools, umbrellas, phone chargers, loose change, and the like in their cars where convenience is valued over security.

Data classification applies similar risk management concepts. You determine the value of the data, risk tolerance, the necessary convenience, and how much it is worth spending to decrease the risk to an acceptable level.

Few commercial organizations attempt this on any level. Every company should at least be able to identify what I like to call C.E.L.E., information that if leaked would be a Company-Extinction Level Event. Yet, most organizations have not specifically identified the highest level of information, never mind considered where it is stored or how it is transmitted.

This astounds me, as the U.S. government has had a formal classification system since before WWII.[9] It is not a new idea. And while there may be issues in its execution (over classification, vetting process, outdated security procedures, and so forth), the system at least attempts to mark data with an importance level and treat it accordingly. Commercial companies must do the same to prioritize their efforts.

Step 4 is to prioritize the user base by the sensitivity of the data they can access. This follows directly from understanding the importance of the underlying data in Step 3. Unless there are sufficient penalties and incentives, all the policy in the world will be steamrolled by business expediency. Instead of blaming users, proactively identify those with the most access and earmark them for a higher level of scrutiny.

Step 5 is to prioritize systems according to how they interact on the network. For example, if people on the HR network routinely receive attachments in e-mail, that is, resumes, then apply a higher level of security designed to prevent initial access to that network.

The goal of these five steps is to understand the key points of the organization, the high ground, as it were, that must be secured. Not every user, system, and byte of data needs to be prioritized in the first pass. This must be an ongoing process lest the organization get bogged down in cataloging everything and thereby never actually improving security.

Penetration testing can also be useful for identifying key weak points. Penetration done right that is. A two-week scan of external servers using commercially available tools is not a penetration test. It's a box-checking exercise, also known as a waste of money.

A true penetration test has no restrictions beyond privacy issues mandated by law and "don't take down the network." It allows time for social engineering and reverse engineering of exposed applications. I have yet to see a true penetration test fail to turn up multiple critical security issues. But even if a penetration test were to fail, it would still be useful to see the network through an Attacker's eyes.

After the initial pass through these steps is complete, the Defender should have a good idea of what needs to be protected and the most likely avenues of access. This is not an easy or a trivial process, but determining and characterizing what is worth protecting is essential.

Now it is time to evaluate options and create a specific plan of action. For this task, Defenders should apply the strategic principles as a framework for evaluating specific defensive tactics.

A couple of guiding thoughts for any tactic:

- Implement any changes swiftly and across complete network segments so as to minimize the Attacker's ability to react.

- Establish typical user scenarios and roles for any defensive restriction so as to force Attackers to violate normal usage to accomplish their tasks.

Following is an evaluation of items from the Australian Defense Signals Directory "Strategies to Mitigate Targeted Cyber Intrusions,"[10] an excellent guide. A given organization may evaluate this list and come to different conclusions than those proffered. However, the point is that the effect on the Attacker's strategy is paramount in determining whether an idea is worth the cost.

To review: the five categories of defensive actions that break the offensive operational life cycle from Chapter 3 are

- *Privacy* manages the publishing of information to countertargeting.

- *Prevention* stops initial access or persistence.

- *Constraint* limits lateral movement within a network.

- *Obstruction* impedes data exfiltration.

- *Detection* is the catchall for finding and recognizing the Attacker during any part of the operational life cycle.

The test of any tactic is whether it reliably accomplishes some aspect of one or more of these.

Application Whitelisting

Application whitelisting is a technical constraint that enables only certain known good programs to run, that is, programs on the whitelist. All other programs are blocked by default. It's like throwing a house party and allowing only people in that you recognize. Anyone you don't recognize is blocked.

Whitelisting is in contrast to blacklisting where by default, all programs are allowed to run except those explicitly forbidden. In the case of our house party, the doors are swung wide open, unless the person is specifically on the bad list.

A perfect whitelisting system would be effective. It forces the Attacker to have a priori awareness of the environment and prevents the installation of backdoors or the deployment of tools. It requires new innovation to circumvent.

Think of the iPhone App Store. Apple has instituted the requirement that all software must be submitted to them for examination before it is allowed to run on their platform. This has made running malicious software much more difficult, though notably not impossible. No perfect system exists.

Even still, this is a special case. Not all platforms are as tightly controlled, nor can they be. Companies develop and run their own software for their own needs. Imagine having to clear your company's new e-commerce site and back end inventory tracking system through Apple before allowing it to be deployed. It is not going to happen.

The effectiveness of more general whitelisting solutions depends greatly on the implementation. The most common tactic to circumvent one is to coerce an allowed program to load and execute alien code. In fact, there is an entire class of vulnerabilities called "Dll hijacking" that involve tricking other programs, presumably whitelisted ones, into running malicious code. (Of course, there are also defensive solutions that protect against this.)

Other tricks involve using scriptable engines, such as Windows PowerShell, to do the dirty work. An administrator is often left with the option of either whitelisting these engines and accepting the risk, or not whitelisting them and having to rely on something less convenient.

Yet despite its flaws, whitelisting still forces Attacker knowledge, awareness, and innovation. In addition, even imperfect solutions allow Defenders to focus their attention on strengthening the whitelisting mechanism and culling the allowable program list, rather than having to worry about dynamically categorizing every conceivable download.

Whitelisting solutions are ideal for anywhere with a semistatic configuration: libraries, ATMs, cash registers, and so on. They are less effective in dynamic environments, such as software development or IT management, which require installing and running a large variety of tools. Again, if it gets in the way of productivity, it will not last long.

In short, if there is a way to effectively deploy this without impeding the user base, then application whitelisting directly affects the Attacker's strategy.

Network Segmentation and Segregation

Network segmentation and segregation consists of dividing the network into logical or functional units. Common segmentations include cutting up the network by city, by building, by department, or ideally by security zones. The theory is that divisions can stop the Attacker from leveraging a foothold in one segment into access in another segment.

Segmentation limits the potential damage of a compromise to whatever is in that one segment. It emphasizes the Defender's asymmetric advantage of knowing the network terrain. It effectively divides one target into many.

The Attacker is left with two choices: treat each segment as a separate network, or compromise one and attempt to jump the divide. Neither choice is appealing.

Treating each segment as a separate network creates a great deal more work. It requires gaining initial access to each segment, establishing reliable communications, and going through all the other stages of the operational life cycle. This sucks away resources. This approach also dramatically increases Attackers' exposure, which hits their ability to remain operationally secure.

If instead Attackers try to jump between segments, it exposes a different chink in their operational security. If the segments are designed well, then the network traffic between them can be restricted. There are always exceptions that must be allowed through, such as communication with domain servers for centralized account management, but this limited traffic is easier to characterize. When the Attacker has to cross these segments, it creates the perfect choke point, a digital Thermopylae, as it were. Put in a few Spartans, or some well-configured network monitoring, and the invading army of Xerxes will at least be spotted.

Therefore, if network segmentation is paired with network boundary monitoring, it effectively constrains the Attacker's ability to move and obstructs their ability to communicate. It counters their strategy of operational security.

Segmentation is also useful to the extent it enables data classification. Each segment can be set at a different level of security and monitored appropriately. Overall, segmentation is just a good idea.

Centralized…Logging of…Computer Events with Automated, Immediate Log Analysis

This sounds great on paper. Record suspicious logins and other computer events and look for anomalies. It is certainly useful to reconstruct what happened during an attack after the fact, but it is of questionable value for preventing one.

Unless logging is tailored to specific systems or choke points, it is of little use. There are rarely logs during the initial intrusion, so logging will not detect when the Attacker first lands. So beyond initial access, it becomes a question of whether Attacker actions will trigger an alert.

The problem is Attackers can systematically determine the time or numeric thresholds for triggering alerts and augment their operational security to stay below that threshold. How? By setting aside one sacrificial computer; trying stuff out; and then monitoring what happens if alerts are generated, if a person logs in, or if access to that computer is lost.

After the Attacker gains a certain level of awareness of how the system works, they will sidestep logging entirely, or just ignore it. Attacker actions were logged when they penetrated Target and they were with Home Depot. That still didn't stop me from having to get a new credit card. Centralized logging is generally too little too late. It does not force any innovation or changes to operational security.

What it does do is give the Defender something to look at after a compromise. This may help with disseminating information and increasing the cost of program security, but usually, centralized logging does not effectively counter the Attacker's strategy.

Web Domain Whitelisting for All Domains

Web domain whitelisting is similar to application whitelisting. Users are limited to browsing only those websites that are on the list of explicitly approved sites.

Whitelisting helps in two ways. First, it limits the avenues of infiltration. If users cannot go to untrusted websites, they are less vulnerable. There are various ways around this, such as exploiting advertising networks to deliver Attacker code, but it's a solid 80 percent solution for stopping initial access via the web.

Second, whitelisting helps by limiting Attackers' options for communication after they establish access. The Attacker must use a different protocol, compromise an upstream router, perform a positional access operation, or otherwise directly attack the whitelisting mechanism to communicate. It creates a clear obstruction.

To overcome web domain whitelisting, the Attackers need knowledge of the whitelisting mechanism and awareness of the implementation. Neither is trivial.

Where it falls apart is in practice. Imagine if every time an engineer tried to look up a product spec, or a marketer attempted to see competitor products, or an HR manager looked at salary information, there was some hoop to jump through. The number of people who will require exceptions is enormous. And those are for legitimate business reasons. In reality, this policy will be tested the first time the manager tries to check his kid's school's website to see if snow is causing an early closing or to look up his dentist's phone number. People have come to expect unmitigated access to the Internet.

A website whitelisting policy, although great in theory, is difficult to implement. It goes against the foundational principle of humanity. For this reason, it is unlikely to be effective in any but the most constrained scenarios.

Deny Direct Internet Access from Workstations...[and] Force Traffic Through a Split DNS Server, an E-mail Server, or an Authenticated Web Proxy

Parsing the technical jargon, this basically means that all outbound access is routed through an authenticating choke point where access can be controlled and monitored as shown in Figure 8.2.

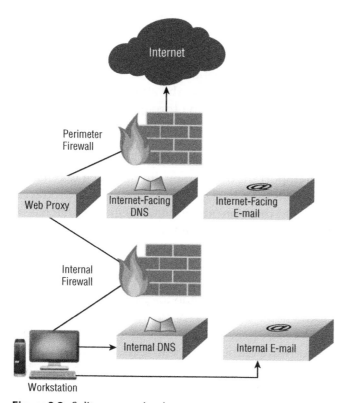

Figure 8.2: Split server and web proxy setup

The split e-mail server setup means that even if Attackers compromises the external server, they still will not have access to intracompany e-mails. The split DNS server prevents similar types of problems.

The authenticated web proxy is probably the most important part. It helps ensure that a live person is driving the outbound connection and not some unknown program.

This setup should be the first thing on everyone's to-do list. It severely limits the methods of access. It is economical. There may be up-front work required to reconfigure the network into this architecture, but when done, it requires few resources to maintain. It has practically no impact on the user base and therefore is unlikely to generate any pushback.

This configuration forces innovation. It limits the options for precaution as people can lock down which communication methods are allowed out. It punishes a lack of awareness with complete loss of access. It raises the level of operational security required, as there is a single choke point the Defender can monitor.

A split network architecture with authentication is not impenetrable, but it accomplishes quite a lot for little investment. It directly counters the Attacker's strategy on almost every level.

Other Strategies

The preceding examples are simplified evaluations. I could write more about the advantages of each, the attacks they prevent, the attacks they allow, the likelihood of successful implementation including through maintenance and updates, and the impact on the user base. And all those factors will be different for each organization.

In addition, these five strategies are a small percentage of the strategies the Defender must evaluate. The important thing in evaluating each defensive method is to factor in how it impacts the Attacker's strategy. Antivirus products have minimal strategic impact and therefore are doomed. Segmentation has a large impact and therefore should be implemented for any medium-to-large network.

Even dynamic processes, such as incident response, can benefit from examination in the context of strategic principles.

For example, a common incident response methodology looks for the point of initial access and then for where the intruders spread, noting what data was compromised. The more technical response teams meticulously reverse engineer every piece of Attacker software encountered and learn how it works. In the end, the Defender often simply cleans up the affected systems, closes the vulnerability that allowed initial access (if possible), and calls it a day.

By all means, the Defender should determine the point of initial access and close it. But rather than focus on the Attacker's software, you should focus on how it was deployed. Were administrative accounts used? Were they used after hours or in another anomalous manner? What awareness systems could be put in place to detect this type of usage? This type of evaluation puts countering the Attackers' methodology and forcing changes to their operational security over detecting a specific piece of software they deployed.

Another more cost-effective follow-up than reverse engineering might be to assume that everything on the entire network segment is compromised and toast it. Already the more security-conscious business travelers I know (myself included) do this on an individual level before going to high-risk places like the security conference DEFCON or China. My checklist includes the following steps:

- Take a backup of my laptop.
- Wipe it of all information or install from a clean image.
- Travel.
- Wipe laptop of all information upon return.
- Change any passwords used while traveling.
- Restore from backup.

One executive I know even goes so far as to purchase a new laptop every time he travels to China, figuring a cheap laptop costs roughly one quarter the cost of the airfare alone.

Now buying new computers for the entire network is not feasible, but there are actions that are. If reloading an entire network segment seems daunting, then think about how technologies such as virtualization, rapid image deployment, and so on could automate it and make it easy. With such a system in place, an administrator could start doing it randomly throughout the network before a compromise. This eviscerates precaution and requires the Attacker to have even more awareness to avoid losing access.

Admittedly this strategy is useless in a "bring your own device" environment. That invites a whole different set of problems. But the solutions will still need to be considered in the context of offensive principles.

There is no shortage of issues and a lot of sound advice out there, but with the proper evaluation and tailoring, a defensive strategy can be crafted to directly counter the Attacker's strategy.

Cloud-Based Security

The Cloud is the latest in a long series of ambiguous marketing buzzwords. It basically means there is some network of computers that perform some tasks for the client. There are some technical advances behind virtualizing computers and making resources available on demand, but at its core, cloud computing is an old concept that has been around since the mainframes of the 1950s.

Some computers, located somewhere that is network accessible, do stuff. That's it. "Stuff" can be storing and backing up data. It can be provisioning a new piece of infrastructure or a fully configured server. It can be serving up an application on demand.

The phrase *cloud-based security* can refer to two different things. The first is the security of the cloud service provider. How secure is the data it holds on your behalf? What are the access controls? Is data stored encrypted? The fundamental problems of computer security are the same. It just puts them in someone else's hands.

This form of cloud-based security has some advantages. Providers such as Amazon Web Services, Rackspace, and Microsoft have enormous resources and expertise they can bring to bear on the problem. Any security enhancements they might apply instantly improve the security of their entire client base.

There are also some disadvantages. It opens up new potential vulnerabilities, such as the connection between the cloud provider and the client. Environments an enterprise has no control over and vulnerabilities they have never considered, such as breaking out of a virtualized environment or hypervisor-based rootkits, suddenly and invisibly become critical to security. It also creates a bigger, more lucrative target. If the provider is compromised, every one of their clients is potentially compromised.

Only time will tell whether relying on a third-party provider for security is ultimately better or worse. Either way, while it shifts the responsibility for defending, it does not change anything about defensive strategy.

The second and perhaps more interesting meaning of cloud-based security is one in which security decisions are instantly reviewed "in the cloud." In this usage, *cloud* means information is transmitted to the security provider for analysis, and some result or recommendation of action is sent back.

The concept is potentially an effective defensive strategy that can impact the Attacker's ability to operate. Cloud-based security can implement most of the advantages of application whitelisting while removing the disadvantage of inflexibility. It can remove the knowledge requirement from each individual user or each organization and put the burden on the industry. The security provider can search across all of their customers and see if this program or this behavior has been encountered before and tailor their action depending on the results. No more dialog boxes popping up asking if some action is okay. The provider already knows if it's okay with a high degree of confidence.

A cloud-based strategy also rebalances an asymmetry by removing the Attacker's ability to pretest software against the system. Instead of having to push out new signatures, the security providers can simply alter how decisions are made within their cloud. This is difficult to test against without potentially leaking offensive information.

It reintroduces the friction of uncertainty into the Attackers' actions, or at minimum, it increases the burden of continual testing. Innovation and awareness are made more difficult as the target is effectively fluid. Cloud-based security decreases program security as information is automatically shared between targets. It also increases the friction of updates because patches to the system will be deployed instantly.

Taken together, these points make cloud-based security an effective counter to the Attacker's strategy. Of course, nothing is perfect. This requires a connection to the provider, something not always feasible and that in itself may open up new vulnerabilities.

Also no plan survives contact with the enemy. The Attacker will adapt. Possible approaches include finding and exploiting vulnerabilities in the security software, sidestepping deployments, or going after the security company directly.

The last two tactics are exactly what Attackers did to circumvent Bit9, a self-proclaimed cloud-based software reputation service.

> *Due to an operational oversight within Bit9, we failed to install our own product on a handful of computers within our network. As a result, a malicious third party was able to illegally gain temporary access to one of our digital code-signing certificates that they then used to illegitimately sign malware.*[11]
>
> **—Bit9 Press Release, February 2013**

Although it is easy to cast stones at Bit9 for its failure, that misses the larger point. It is a welcome strategic shift if the Attacker becomes routinely forced into attacking a computer security company to be successful. In this case, the Attacker is compelled to ignore an age-old tenet of any conflict.

> *So in war, the way is to avoid what is strong and to strike at what is weak.*[12]
>
> **—Sun Tzu**

The Attacker was relegated to striking at what is strong, a computer security company, one that has an overwhelming business incentive to remain secure. Security may have failed in this one case, but it did so by forcing the Attacker to perform a positional access operation against a more prepared opponent. The defensive strategy was sound. It was just the execution that was flawed.

The future will likely play out with Attackers attempting to find new and creative ways to exempt themselves from inspection, either by directly attacking security companies by seeding the cloud (that is, getting malicious software put on the okay list), or by some other method.

The Attacker may succeed at combating cloud-based security to an extent, but at least the dynamics of the Attackers' strategy will be forcibly altered, something that has not actually happened yet.

Summary

Evaluating potential strategies according to the strategic principles enables people to recognize their practical and theoretical limitations and their systemic strengths and weaknesses. With this understanding, individual solutions can be fit together to craft a resilient defensive strategy.

In the next chapter, we'll examine some notable real-world case studies and attempt to derive and critique the offensive strategies employed.

Offensive Case Studies

I don't care if I pass your test, I don't care if I follow your rules.
If you can cheat, so can I. I won't let you beat me
unfairly—I'll beat you unfairly first.

—Andrew Wiggin, *Ender's Game*

The goal of an operation is usually straightforward to determine. Indeed, this is what the media focuses on: the number of stolen credit cards, the amount of cash taken from ATMs, this or that product design, and so forth.

The means of an operation can also be recovered. It is not always easy, but a team of skilled forensic analysts can ordinarily determine how an organization was compromised. This is what security companies tend to focus on: the initial vulnerability exploited, the signatures of the programs used, the communication protocols employed, the addresses of the command and control servers, and if possible, who the Attackers are.

What's historically been missing from these analyses is an understanding of how Attackers systematically create and leverage the means to achieve their goals. The strategy is absent.

This is for good reason. Attackers actively obscure their strategy, not to mention their budgets and staffing levels. You can find and analyze the proverbial "pointy end of the spear" sticking into the gut of your organization, but that sheds little light on the location of the iron ore mine, the steel forging process, and the soldier training regimen that allows Attackers to fashion and wield that spear so effectively.

Unless, of course, you witness the evolution of that spear over time or across multiple targets. Then, perhaps, a few bits of strategy can be inferred. Fortunately, a few such high-profile examples exist.

The cases in this chapter have undergone extensive technical analysis by capable individuals and companies. The cases have much in common, as they must, because all operations follow the life cycle detailed in Chapter 2 , "The Attacker,": targeting, initial access, expansion, exfiltration (or destruction), and detection.

Yet each example betrays at least one unique aspect and sometimes more. By focusing on these differences, you can see how Attackers' strategies fit within the proposed framework.

Stuxnet

Stuxnet is the world's most reported example of *computer network attack (CNA)*. First found in 2010, the malware infiltrated the computers and equipment used to control Iranian nuclear centrifuges. But unlike most computer infiltrations, the code was not designed to steal information. Instead, the program subtly and occasionally manipulated infected centrifuge controllers to cause the centrifuge to physically break.[1] The aggregate effect was to slow the entire Iranian nuclear program.

Stuxnet is not the first example of physical harm caused through software. According to Thomas Reed in *At the Abyss: An Insider's History of the Cold War,*[2] the U.S. engineered a natural gas pipeline explosion in Siberia in 1982 by allowing the Soviets to steal defective designs and faulty control software.

Nor was Stuxnet the most noxious attack. That honor belongs to an incident in 2000 in Queensland, Australia, in which an aggrieved former employee used insider knowledge and a radio link to access sewage control systems. (I use the word "access" as opposed to "compromise" because there was no real defensive security to speak of.) The soon-to-be-arrested perpetrator released hundreds of thousands of gallons of raw sewage into the environment.

Stuxnet may not even be the first physical attack executed by means of infecting a network. Recent reporting suggests an oil pipeline in Turkey was sabotaged in 2008 by first compromising (you'll love this) the security cameras and using those to tunnel into the network.

What sets Stuxnet apart is the planning, engineering, and depth of technical expertise required. To pull this off, the Stuxnet authors employed almost every strategic principle.

Access

The Iranian enrichment plant at Natanz had no Internet access as far as we know. It was a completely isolated network. Physical access was presumably tightly controlled via gates, guards, badges, and such. Yet, the Attacker managed to penetrate a network that required physical access without setting a foot in the country. How exactly? Through the facility's suppliers.

Symantec first tracked five organizations as the initial Stuxnet infection vectors.[3] Kaspersky later identified them in a blog post entitled "Stuxnet: Victims Zero."[4] Unsurprisingly, the five companies dealt with the creation of things the facility required: industrial control software, machinery, and materials.

It is unclear which company served as the way in or if multiple did. Or perhaps the Attacker had a paid informant or some other means of circumventing physical security. Regardless, the penetration of a highly monitored nuclear facility again demonstrates that there is always a method of access.

Economy

Stuxnet was built with a modular architecture. As detailed in Chapter 7, "Offensive Strategy," this type of architecture offers major efficiencies in resource use. Since Stuxnet targeted such a diverse array of technologies, ranging from USB drives Windows computers and to embedded controllers, breaking the effort it took into separate but compatible development pieces was the most economical approach.

Humanity

Whether it was a vendor that brought in an outside laptop, an engineer that installed an untrusted update, a scientist that used a thumb drive between secure systems, or a paid insider, gaining and expanding access exploited the human elements. Stuxnet would not have succeeded without a thorough understanding of how technical security measures could be overcome by human failings.

Knowledge

Just as the character Marty McFly noted in the classic movie *Back to the Future*, "Doc, you don't just walk into a store and buy plutonium," you can't stop by the local Home Depot to get a uranium enrichment device. And yet, Attackers obtained and leveraged deep knowledge of the IR-1 centrifuge internals: its design, spin tolerances, pressure flows, the possible cascade setups, and more.

They also knew the architecture, programming languages, and project structures of Siemen's programmable logic controllers (PLCs), the specific devices that communicated with the centrifuges. Beyond this, Attackers had extensive knowledge of Windows vulnerability discovery and exploitation.

Any one of these topics might take someone years to learn and master. Together, they represent decades of accumulated expertise. Attackers behind Stuxnet had no shortage of knowledge.

Awareness

Attackers had static awareness of the operational domain. They understood which companies were linked to their ultimate target. They knew the specific hardware the target used. They knew the specific cascade setup and the frequencies it operated at. All this can be seen in the specificity of the payloads. I would not be surprised if they knew the names and schedules of the Iranian technicians and what they liked for breakfast.

How Attackers acquired this awareness is unknown. Perhaps the previously infiltrated industrial companies had this information on their networks. Perhaps there was a configuration error and parts of the facility were connected to the Internet at one point. Perhaps an engineer used a compromised laptop to connect to both the internal network and his home network, effectively providing a bridge between the two. Maybe there were informants. It's hard to say.

However it was done, it seems unlikely that the Attackers gained awareness in real time. The Stuxnet worm, after it infiltrated Natanz, could not communicate home. So how did Attackers compensate for this weakness? They exercised extreme precaution.

Precaution

With no dynamic awareness to rely on, and limited opportunities for altering course, the Stuxnet authors had to prepare for every reasonable contingency. And so they did.

The worm contained two privilege escalation exploits: one for Windows XP and prior, and one for Windows Vista and later. It did not matter which Windows operating system the Iranians were running, or even if they upgraded them sequentially while the attack was ongoing. The worm would still gain privileged access.

It also checked for and tailored its behavior to avoid most major antivirus programs including those produced by Kaspersky, McAfee, Symantec, Bitdefender, F-Secure, ESET, and TrendMicro. (To avoid these products, Stuxnet would inject into and commandeer the running process of the product, essentially removing itself from scrutiny.) Given the large variety of products specifically targeted, Attackers must not have been certain which was installed. So they covered the proverbial 90 percent of the market.

Attackers also defended against updates applied to the lowest components, the Siemen's PLCs. Any update to an already Trojaned PLC would be intercepted and co-opted before it could be applied, ensuring that the PLC would remain infected.

The worm used multiple ways to spread. The most reliable method relied on a 0-day exploit to jump from one machine to another. However, if some day that were patched, Stuxnet could also spread through using network file shares, a legitimate network feature that could not be patched.

Stuxnet also used multiple ways to update itself or receive new commands. If by luck it could connect to the Internet, Stuxnet could reach out to a command and control servers for new commands. But if not, the malware could receive updates via a peer-to-peer network, meaning from other Stuxnets. The Attackers needed to get only one instance to update, and that update would get propagated throughout the entire network.

At every step of the operation, Stuxnet employed diversity and redundancy to guard against unwitting actions. This extreme precaution more than compensated for any lack of awareness.

Innovation

Stuxnet contained a number of technical innovations. The authors created a rootkit to provide stealth on PLCs, something that to my knowledge has never been done before or since.

It circumvented every major antivirus program. This is by no means a new concept, but it can be difficult to do in practice. Other innovations such as modular architecture, dynamic updates, safeguards to prevent spreading, and more are also established concepts, but the Stuxnet team's integration and implementation were unprecedented.

The worm contained four different 0-day vulnerabilities: one to get installed, one to spread, and two to elevate privileges. Using a 0-day vulnerability is not innovative by itself; every professional offensive organization uses them. The true innovation here, beyond finding or acquiring them in the first place, was seamlessly linking the four together to create something universal—an exploit chain to rule them all.

The list of technical innovations goes on and on. But if innovation is the transformation of an industry or a way of thinking, then the true innovation of Stuxnet was not technical but operational. Stuxnet reached in and remotely touched something purposefully disconnected from the world and caused it to physically break.

As Dave Aitel put it, the message of Stuxnet is that "I can take out any factory you have at any time I choose."[5] This simple message, when finally heeded, will transform how our entire society views CNE. The technical innovations of Stuxnet will be overshadowed, but the psychological impact of it will remain.

Operational Security

At the end of the day, Stuxnet was caught, so on a black-and-white scale, operational security failed. But it's more nuanced than that. It's not that Stuxnet was operationally insecure, just that it succumbed to undefeatable frictions: flawed attack tools and bad luck.

Stuxnet leveraged many forms of operational security. First and foremost it did not immediately destroy every centrifuge that it reached. If it had, the Iranians would have immediately suspected sabotage and gone looking for the source.

If the goal was to slow the surreptitious nuclear program, and by all accounts it was, then a total cascade failure would perversely be a less consequential setback. Iran would root out the Attackers and rebuild cleanly, ever the more wary. A more operationally secure approach was to bleed the program slowly—and hopefully for indecipherable reasons.

The program minimized its exposure by exploiting what is supposed to be a trusted outside process, digital signing. A digital signature, like a regular signature, is used to identify the author of a piece of software. Signatures are created from certificates, which are granted by a Certificate Authority after a certain level of due diligence. (In the United States, a business may need to provide a DUNS number, a copy of its business license, copies of bills, tax ID numbers, and other information to receive a certificate.)

Stuxnet installed a driver, a piece of software that interacts directly with the underlying operating system. Drivers are not inherently malicious; they are needed to communicate with hardware, such as a network card, and by antivirus companies to seek out malicious high-level behavior. However, drivers run with full privileges and can be malicious and manipulate core operating system functions to hide files, processes, network connections, and more. Because of the potential for this malicious behavior, Microsoft (as of Windows Vista) requires all drivers to be signed, relying on the scrutiny of the certificate process to weed out nefarious actors.

Antivirus products, at least the ones in 2010, employed a similar model. Anything signed was treated with a higher degree of trust. Attackers exploited this trust by signing their payload, but rather than undergo scrutiny to obtain a certificate, they saved themselves the annoyance and instead stole certificates from two Chinese hardware companies and used theirs. This killed two birds with one stone; it circumvented various defensive protections and also supplied a level of misdirection should anyone examine the drivers.

Stuxnet drivers were rootkits, programs designed to provide stealth, and when installed, they put chosen files and processes beyond the reach of antivirus software. But there was another component that needed protection, the modified code that ran on the Siemen's PLC. To hide this, Attackers produced the world's first known PLC rootkit, a program that hooked the Siemen's control software and scrubbed any evidence of the modified code from any query results. This took operational security to a whole new level of depth.

Beyond hiding its components, Stuxnet also employed methods to stop it from spreading too far. Reportedly, this component was flawed:

> *An error in the code, they said, had led it to spread to an engineer's computer when it was hooked up to the centrifuges. When the engineer left Natanz and connected the computer to the Internet, the American- and Israeli-made bug failed to recognize that its environment had changed. It began replicating itself all around the world. Suddenly, the code was exposed, though its intent would not be clear, at least to ordinary computer users.*[6]

> —*The New York Times*

This spreading led to its eventual discovery. Once discovered, there was little the Attacker could do to follow another tenet of operational security, preventing recognition.

No doubt Attackers hoped their program would get lost in the noise of the thousands of pieces of malware found every day. Some have suggested that some parts were intentionally less sophisticated for this very reason. Regardless, luck was not on the Attacker's side. A researcher at Symantec took an interest in it, initiating its eventual demise.

Though the operation was eventually exposed, the Attackers behind Stuxnet took great pains to be operationally secure. The ultimate uncovering in no way lessens the work and benefits that went into adhering to this strategic principle. As Kim Zetter wrote:

> There were so many things that had to go wrong for Stuxnet and its arsenal of tools to be discovered and deciphered that it's a wonder any of it occurred.[7]
>
> —*Countdown to Zero Day*

A wonder indeed.

Program Security

The program security of Stuxnet was a mixed success. On attribution, the technical analysis of Stuxnet held out and was ambiguous. Some concluded it must have been U.S. and/or Israeli backed given the purported target and the depth of knowledge and sophistication. But apart from a few tidbits here and there, there was no smoking gun in the details.

However, any veil of anonymity or plausible deniability that might have existed was shredded by leaks from various unnamed U.S. government sources taking credit. Now there's even an "Operation Olympic Games," the alleged code name for the operation, on Wikipedia.

Of course, these leaks could have been a thought-out policy decision. Some have suggested a similar motive for a far more destructive weapon.

> In the years since the two atomic bombs were dropped on Japan, a number of historians have suggested that the weapons had a two-pronged objective. First, of course, was to bring the war with Japan to a speedy end and spare American lives. It has been suggested that the second objective was to demonstrate the new weapon of mass destruction to the Soviet Union.[8]
>
> —**History.com**

Likewise, there may have been a dual objective with Stuxnet: slow the nuclear program, but if caught, send a message and instill some fear and paranoia. Or maybe some people just can't keep secrets. Either way, the Attackers' identity is widely suspected. But as mentioned in Chapter 4, "Asymmetries," attribution is not necessarily earth shattering when it comes to nation states.

Though Attacker anonymity seems pierced, Stuxnet did have some clear program security successes.

There was no immediate target pollution. Thousands of other infections were found and cleared, but these seem more likely to be instances of the potent worm gone wild rather than deliberate targets. The one exception is the original five implanted companies that served as infection vectors. Whatever intelligence value these organizations may have had beyond serving as an infection vector was probably lost, but I don't see how that could have been handled any differently.

Defenders did eventually discover another offensive software platform, dubbed Duqu, and that platform contained enough in common with Stuxnet that they were able to link the two to the same authors. But it took 2 years to find it, even with Stuxnet in hand, so I'd regard that as an offensive success.

On the clear program security failure side, a large and rather valuable cache of technical vulnerabilities, tools, and methodologies were burned when Stuxnet was exposed. Estimates put the development of Stuxnet in the millions of dollars, and much of that went up in smoke.

Yet just because program security failed does not mean the Attackers were ignorant of the principle. The degree of development, planning, and execution suggests the opposite. Rather, my guess is the Attackers considered the costs, the blowback of attribution, the value of the exploits, the lost platform, the infrastructure, and the potential exposure of other operations and found the benefits of mission success outweighed them.

Stuxnet Summary

The component ideas of Stuxnet (worms, 0-day exploits, rootkits, and such) all predate the worm by decades. With the exception of the PLC rootkit, no individual piece is particularly special. But Stuxnet as an attack is. Why? Because this was the first public insight into a well-planned offensive operation, one that duly considered strategic principles for its execution.

Flame

Flame is another software espionage platform. Like Stuxnet, the Flame platform consisted of a modular architecture that allowed plug-ins for expanded functionality, conserving development resources by providing a common base of functionality.

Also like Stuxnet, the set of targets were primarily in Iran, though Flame concentrated on espionage instead of sabotage. Is this just a coincidence? Doubtful.

Later analysis revealed that an early version of Stuxnet had a Flame module in it.[9] This leads to a couple possible conclusions.

1. Either Flame came first OR there is still an earlier version of Stuxnet out there that does not include the module.

2. Either the authors of Stuxnet coordinated with Flame's authors OR they captured and repurposed it.

Although the answer is surely interesting to know for geopolitical reasons, the key point is that Flame and Stuxnet are different. There may or may not have been coordination, but the development teams were separate.

Flame had a few particularly telling characteristics that demonstrate strategic principles. First, the team invested heavily in knowledge and innovation.

All Microsoft Windows computers run something called Windows Update. This software periodically reaches out to Microsoft, checks the update level of the operating system, and downloads and installs the appropriate updates.

To save on bandwidth costs and accommodate various secure network setups where client computers cannot connect to the Internet, Microsoft allows companies to set up their own internal Windows Update server, as shown in Figure 9.1. The Windows Update server downloads updates from Microsoft and caches them locally. Then, computers inside the network pull and apply updates from the server.

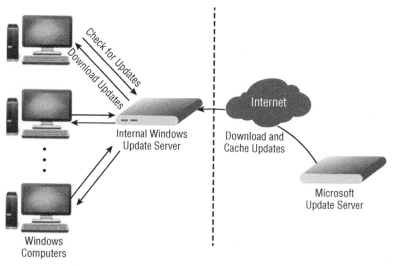

Figure 9.1: Internal Windows Update server

Flame corrupted this process. Flame spread by converting an infected computer into an internal Windows Update server and then advertising it to the network[10], as shown in Figure 9.2.

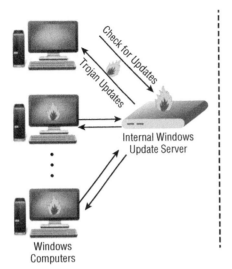

Check for Updates

Trojan Updates

Internal Windows
Update Server

Windows
Computers

Figure 9.2: Flame internal Windows Update server

Whenever another computer on the same network needed an update, it would contact the infected computer. This demonstrates a detailed knowledge of the update system, but it is not enough to spread a malicious update. To prevent exactly this sort of rogue update server, Microsoft digitally signs all updates using a code signing certificate. Client computers verify this signature before applying an update.

To circumvent this protection, the Flame authors had to make their update appear to be signed by Microsoft. Describing this feat would require diving into an explanation of certificates, digital signatures, Microsoft Terminal Services licensing, and more. But suffice it to say that through a combination of a detailed understanding of the signing process, advanced cryptography, brute force computing power, and incredible timing (less than 1 millisecond room for error), the authors of Flame forged a Microsoft code signing certificate, which gave it the ability to sign anything.

The Flame espionage malware that infected computers in Iran achieved mathematic breakthroughs that could only have been accomplished by world-class cryptographers. . . .[11]

–Ars Technica

With this enormous power, the infected update server could serve up anything the Attacker wanted, and any computer that used it as the server would install it. Flame spread throughout a network at will without compromising a single password or exploiting a vulnerability. This is the definition of innovation.

Next, the Attacker was keenly aware of all potential targets of the operation:

[T]he team behind Flame launched their cleanup about ten days before news of Flame broke. . . . The Kaspersky researchers had likely tipped them off inadvertently when they connected a test machine infected with Flame to the internet. As soon as the machine went online, the malware reached out to one of Flame's command servers. . . . In a panic, they wiped the command servers and sent out a kill module. . . .[7]

—Countdown to Zero Day

This was no watering hole attack with random victims. The command and control team must have scrutinized every new instance to recognize an anomaly so quickly. Its reaction demonstrates vigilance to awareness and operational security.

Finally, Flame vastly increased the cost of analysis to improve program security.

Flame also goes to great lengths to obscure itself. . . . Instead of seeing a function call that's the computer equivalent to "snoop around this person's contact list," researchers initially see what appear to be random characters.[12]

—Digital Trends

As for what this means for analysts:

"It took us half a year to analyze Stuxnet," he said. "This is 20 times more complicated. It will take us 10 years to fully understand everything."[13]

—Alexander Gostev, chief security expert at Kaspersky Lab as reported by *Wired*

Even if Gostev is overestimating the amount of work by 100 percent, in 5 years the authors of Flame could produce countless variations or even an entirely new toolkit from scratch that will avoid whatever detection algorithms the analysts devise.

Flame aptly demonstrates the strategic principles in action.

Gauss

Gauss is a software espionage platform that targeted various entities in the Middle East. It bears substantial resemblance to Flame. In fact, the similarities are how Kaspersky found it.

Based on the results of a detailed analysis of Flame, we continued to actively search for new, unknown components. A more in-depth analysis conducted in June 2012 resulted in the discovery of a new, previously unknown malware platform that uses a modular structure resembling that of Flame, a similar code base and system for communicating to C&C servers, as well as numerous other similarities to Flame.[14]

—Gauss: Abnormal Distribution

Gauss enjoys an advanced repertoire of collection and communication capabilities, but there is one aspect that is particularly remarkable. Gauss contains an encrypted component that is keyed to a specific environment. It is locked on to a specific target.

Gauss derives a decryption key from a system setting and the list of installed programs, as shown in Figure 9.3.

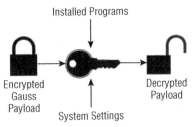

Installed Programs

Encrypted
Gauss
Payload

System Settings

Decrypted
Payload

The compromised system must have the exact configuration necessary to produce the key to decrypt the payload. No one has determined the correct setup yet.

Figure 9.3: Gauss encrypted payload

If the target computer has even a slightly different setup than that chosen by the authors, then nothing is decrypted, and nothing is revealed. To date, no one knows exactly what that environment is, nor has anyone been able to guess or brute force it. The payload remains secure.

Gauss was predominantly found in Lebanon, and other components have collection capabilities against specific Lebanese banks, so it's a safe bet the desired target is somewhere in Lebanon. But beyond that nothing is known. To wit, the Gauss authors employed a strategy of subverting defensive analysis.

This strategy exemplifies several principles. It incorporates knowledge of cryptography and in-depth awareness of the desired target. It introduces a method of operational security that makes any collateral deployments inconsequential. It simply will not do anything on an unintended machine.

Gauss exhibits advanced program security. Finding one version of this component will not help you find another. A separately keyed version could be created for each target, effectively rendering signatures more useless than they already are.

It imposes an economic cost on the Defender. This component cannot be analyzed except on the intended target, which means the Defender needs skilled (and generally expensive) internal resources. Alternatively, the target could call in outside help, but realistically many targets, notably banks and military organizations, are not going to do this due to secrecy concerns.

Finally, subverting defensive analysis economizes Gauss' authors' resources by limiting what is exposed to the Defensive community. There is no need to recreate capabilities if no one can figure out what they are. This one encrypted module, whatever it is, demonstrates an effective use of offensive principles.

Dragonfly

Dragonfly is a professional computer espionage group operating since at least 2011. Alternatively known as Energetic Bear, this group has successfully penetrated more than 1,000 mostly European energy and equipment suppliers. There is no overwhelming evidence as to who the perpetrators are, but they are believed to be of Eastern European and possibly Russian origin.

That's the dry fact-based version and it is somewhat typical of the tone of the defensive community at large. Let's try the same facts put another way.

For at least the past 4 years, some group, but no one can say whom, has had various levels of access and control over the computer networks of the major operators, equipment manufacturers, and suppliers of the critical infrastructure of Europe. Though, according to Symantec, they had "the capability to mount sabotage operations that could have disrupted energy supplies across a number of European countries,"[15] they graciously chose to focus on espionage. In other words, Europe was spared because there was more money in outright theft than in wreaking havoc. (Or perhaps because they were preparing the battleground for later.)

Sound scary? It is.

Dragonfly's strategy was to focus on a specific industry. It is an effective way to economize limited resources. This focus undoubtedly allowed it to multiply the effect of knowledge across targets, and possibly, given some targets may be interconnected in vendor/purchaser relationships, to leverage access and awareness from one target to another.

Their strategy also exploited the human element. Though Dragonfly used many tried-and-true offensive techniques, such as spear phishing, it also was innovative. The group compromised the "update sites for industrial control system (ICS) software producers."[15] As shown in Figure 9.4, the target visits a known site, one it has gone to before, one that is explicitly allowed through the firewall in a secure setup, and initiates the download.

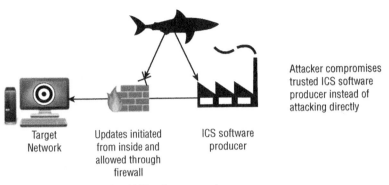

Attacker compromises trusted ICS software producer instead of attacking directly

Target Network

Updates initiated from inside and allowed through firewall

ICS software producer

Figure 9.4: Compromised ICS software producers

It's like when a magician asks you to pick a card. There is an illusion of control. You are picking the card. You pick the site and the software. But even though you think you are in control, you are actually being handed the virtual ace of spades (see Figure 9.5).

Figure 9.5: Pick a card, any card

In short, Dragonfly exploited the human elements and economized resources by focusing on a specific industry. This, in turn, improved the effectiveness of its knowledge, increased its innovation, and improved its operational security. Dragonfly's strategy fits well within the framework.

Red October

Red October is yet another professional multiyear espionage campaign. This one was primarily aimed against government and diplomatic institutions; though some scientific research, nuclear, and aerospace targets were thrown in for good measure.

No one can pinpoint who is behind the group. The targets line up nicely with Russian national interests, and Russian speakers wrote the core software and modules. The exploits, however, are Chinese. Most likely the exploits were purchased or captured, and it's a false flag operation, but in the end, it doesn't matter. The information is gone.

Two aspects of this particular operation stand out. The first is the lengths the Defender, in this case Kaspersky Labs, went to in order to analyze the Attacker. From its report:

> We set up several fake victims around the world and monitored how the attackers handled them over the course of several months. This allowed us to collect hundreds of attack modules and tools. In addition to these, we identified many other modules used in other attacks, which allowed us to gain a unique insight into the attack.[16]

This is a honeypot on a whole new level. It undoes the normal asymmetric advantage the Attacker has in avoiding analysis. It directly counters the principle of awareness and bleeds resources. By setting up multiple victims in disparate locations, Kaspersky witnessed common actions taken across targets without the Attacker realizing it. This is a more strategic way of defending.

The second aspect that stands out is one particular component of the Attacker's toolkit: a third-party plug-in.

To gain initial access, the Red October campaign used targeted e-mails with links or attachments that exploited vulnerabilities in Microsoft Word, Microsoft Excel, or versions of Oracle's Java found in most web browsers. Then it turned that initial access into persistent access by installing malware that beaconed back to command and control servers. So far this is a typical operational pattern.

But then the Attackers did something atypical. They installed their own plug-ins for Microsoft Office and Adobe Reader, extending them with a specialized backdoor of sorts. Whenever the host program was run, the plug-in would load and periodically search through all open files on the system. If any of these files contained a specific marker, the plug-in extracted a hidden payload, decrypted it, and then ran it, or sometimes it would load the code directly into the hosting program.

The plug-in provides a fail-safe. Suppose the primary malware lost the capability to communicate or was found and removed. Further suppose that the vulnerabilities used to gain initial access have been found, fixed, and patched. Finally, perhaps Defenders have improved their security and installed something such as a FireEye Email Security device, which proactively opens attachments and looks for nefarious behavior before allowing them through.

The plug-in enables the Attacker to circumvent all this. If the Attacker can entice the right person to open a (sort of) malicious document, then voilà, they are back in business. The target computer could be fully patched. The document may have been emulated and screened, but it will pass because the document by itself does not do anything. The path to regaining access is that much easier.

The plug-in is also unlikely to attract attention because it rarely does anything. This demonstrates a principle of operational security, breaking up hard-to-link components. I would not be surprised if Kaspersky found this only because they watched it get installed.

Altogether, this simple plug-in shows that Red October Attackers had a firm grasp of operational security and precaution.

APT1

APT1 is a prolific espionage group responsible for hundreds of known intrusions since 2006. Short for Advanced Persistent Threat 1, the group rose to U.S. national prominence with a first-of-its-kind report published by the cyber security company Mandiant titled "APT1: Exposing one of China's Cyber Espionage Units."[17]

Mandiant's report detailed the group's tools, infrastructure, and methodologies, but it went beyond that. It directly linked the group to Chinese state sponsorship. The report provided extensive evidence that APT1 was a unit in the People's Liberation Army of China, specifically the "2nd Bureau of the People's Liberation Army (PLA) General Staff Department's (GSD) 3rd Department, which is most commonly known by its Military Unit Cover Designation (MUCD) as Unit 61398."[17]

Clearly the group failed at maintaining anonymity, a tenet of program security. The report detailed the group's physical location, the estimated number of employees, which university it recruits from, the expected courses of study for graduates, and more, including naming three specific individuals involved.

Attacks are about as fully attributed as any crime can be. Did attribution change anything? Yes and no. The report brought widespread attention to the problem, including testimony before Congress, which may ultimately help spur political action.

But attribution did not stop the Attackers. Mandiant acknowledged as much in its blog post: "APT1 Three Months Later – Significantly Impacted, Though Active & Rebuilding."[18] The technical details of the report, the exposure of infrastructure, and so on may have slowed the group down, but it did not change anything for the medium term. APT1 will be back in full force soon enough, if not already.

So now look at how some of its specific actions fit within the framework.

Once APT1 has established access, they periodically revisit the victim's network over several months or years and steal broad categories of intellectual property, including technology blueprints, proprietary manufacturing processes, test results, business plans, pricing documents, partnership agreements, and e-mails and contact lists from victim organizations' leadership.[17]

—**Mandiant**

The shopping list of items demonstrates a keen focus on attaining full awareness. Business plans, partnership agreements, e-mails and contact lists all yield potential new targets and give some indication of how the company is organized. This is useful from an intelligence perspective and also for maintaining access.

The "periodic" access speaks to operational security. Presumably with each "visit," APT1 did enough to maintain access but avoided doing anything alerting more often than not.

The group also maintained an extensive attack infrastructure with more than 2,500 confirmed fully qualified domain names and an estimated 1,000 servers. (An example of a fully qualified domain name is `evilserver.example.com`.) This conveys a strategy of operational and program security.

With this volume of infrastructure, individual targets can be isolated to separate domains. This prevents discovery and blacklisting of one domain from impacting other operations. The variety of infrastructure also allows APT1 to rotate domains within a given target. One hundred connections to a single domain are a lot more alerting and more likely to be noticed than five connections to twenty domains.

Speaking of which, the domains they chose demonstrated a tenet of operational security, avoiding recognition. Example APT1 domains included

- livemymsn.com
- myhomemsn.com
- myyahoonews.com
- giftwarenews.com
- giftnews.org
- cnndaily.com
- dailycnn.com
- gmailboxes.com

Actually, I lied. Only five out of the eight domains were registered by APT1. The other three are perfectly valid and are owned by the company you might expect. Can you tell the difference? I can't. Your company's security team won't be able to recognize which are malicious either.

APT1 also used less obvious protocols to communicate, such as Jabber (used for various instant messaging programs) and Gmail Calendar. These may not be allowed out of every network, but if they are, what are the odds that they are inspected? Zero.

Like other Attackers, APT1 also demonstrates precaution.

Throughout their stay in the network (which could be years), APT1 usually installs new backdoors as they claim more systems in the environment. Then, if one backdoor is discovered and deleted, they still have other backdoors they can use. We usually detect multiple families of APT1 backdoors scattered around a victim network when APT1 has been present for more than a few weeks.[17]

—Mandiant

APT1 is an anomaly in that the espionage group's nation-state sponsors were identified and called out. But for strategy, it follows and leverages the offensive principles like everyone else.

Axiom

Axiom is another Chinese espionage group targeting—surprise—Western companies and pro-democracy groups (or as China might call them, those that incite subversion of the state). The group was first named in a report released by analytics company Novetta in the Fall of 2014. At a high level, the team seems similar to APT1, just more operationally secure.

Like prior groups, there are a few aspects of Axiom's tradecraft that warrant highlighting.

In many of Axiom's victim environments. . . the total number of malware families leveraged can exceed four separate "layers" of malware. This is likely done to ensure a certain level of persistence and redundant command and control should one of the families ever become compromised.[19]

–Novetta

Four separate malware families? This demonstrates an almost unheard of level of precaution and operational security. Attackers assume they will be detected and plan for it. This directly counters the Defender's usual asymmetric advantage of network awareness and control by making it infeasible to isolate and expunge Attackers. There are too many moving parts to find.

The only effective way for an organization to recover from a compromise like this is to systematically raze its entire network. Cleaning up one computer at a time is not going to cut it. The Attacker will reinfect the machine by the time you can say, "Welcome to Windows." Of course, few organizations can discriminately destroy and rebuild their networks, so this strategy practically guarantees that once Axiom compromises an organization, it is there to stay.

The group's operational security excels in other areas.

The Axiom threat actor group has also demonstrated the operational flexibility of leveraging systems administration tools available within targeted organizations (e.g., Remote Desktop Protocol (RDP), remote administration tools).[19]

–Novetta

Here there aren't even Attacker tools to find. Axiom is simply making use of the administration tools already on the network. Actions like this are next to impossible to detect in logs and must be caught in real time, a drain on the Defender's resources in the best case.

The group also stands out at program security, particularly for infrastructure.

> . . .(*Axiom*) *appear to use a significant amount of C2 infrastructure isolation between targets, with different targets rarely sharing identical C2 locations. This isolation provides a high degree of resiliency … in the event that one operation becomes compromised, other operations are less likely to be interrupted or affected.*[19]
>
> **–Novetta**

Axiom not only compromises intermediaries, but they also purchase infrastructure. Why hack when you can just buy? It shows an evolution in thinking.

The report concludes that "[Axiom's] power comes from their discipline and logistics." It's not from their technological superiority, cunning, cleverness, nor from overwhelming manpower. Its success stems from the development of a sound operational and program security strategy that it strictly follows.

Summary

There are no hard and fast rules in network attacks. Attackers will adapt and use whatever means necessary to achieve their objective. They will "beat you unfairly first." It is therefore difficult to create a universal tactical playbook from case studies. Yet you can see across operations how the Attackers' actions, technologies, and strategies fit into a framework. The tactics will continue to vary and to shift, but the strategy behind them will remain.

Epilogue

The execution of and defense against CNE is vital to our national security, our economy, and our personal privacy and security. Although CNE is a young discipline, it will continue to increase in importance. This book provides a framework for developing the strategies necessary to guide the offensive and defensive actions that will dominate the coming decades of computer security.

I believe that sustained access is and will continue to be the foundation of all offensive operations. Although cyberwar, if it occurs, will be sudden, espionage will remain a game of patience and require the development of long-term capabilities.

The attacking community will continue to be well funded. The sums of money at stake and the national security implications are simply too great. Further, the community will expand to include as-yet undeveloped players, as countries race to keep up with the more technologically advanced by developing or purchasing their own offensive capabilities. The Attackers' collective effectiveness will depend heavily on their professionalism and their ability to conceive and implement strategy.

Meanwhile, though the defensive industry is currently failing quite spectacularly, this is not preordained. The industry must find methods to actively counter offensive principles. Ideas include segmenting communication, inhibiting reverse engineering of defensive products, and rapidly spreading knowledge of methods instead of signatures. These actively counter the principles of precaution, knowledge, and program security, respectively. Any path that does not directly recognize and counter the Attacker's strategy will leave the dynamics of the conflict static, which for the Defender means losing.

Attackers will retain an advantage for the next decade. New espionage campaigns and tools will be stopped and revealed, such as Regin, Turla, and no doubt more before the ink on this book dries, but the balance will remain in the Attackers' favor. The asymmetries and frictions of the space, especially those tied to motivation and focus will require an enormous coordinated effort to overcome. This will be difficult, but it is not impossible.

In 10 to 20 years, I expect the conflict will become more evenly matched. Tolerance for insecurity will plummet as the so-called Facebook generation, with its identities firmly planted in the virtual world, comes to maturity and takes control of company budgets.

A little of this is happening now. When the actress Jennifer Lawrence, of *The Hunger Games* fame, had her personal pictures stolen and sent out across the Internet, she did not react with embarrassment. She reacted with anger at the infiltrators. Other celebrities reacted with anger at the storage providers that allowed it to happen. Almost immediately mobile providers started introducing stronger defensive measures. If enough people get angry, generate enough negative publicity, and start voting for security with their wallets, the nature of the conflict will change.

The societal tipping point will provide funding and motivation for defense at large. How far it tips will depend on the strategy of the defensive community in the coming years. With the proper groundwork, the coming change in perception could be leveraged to great effect.

As the saying goes, "It's tough to make predictions, especially about the future." It's hard to know if the defense can wrest away the initiative. There are just too many variables. In the meantime, as we watch the Attacker/Defender dynamic continue to play out, it is my hope that this book will help those involved make better choices in shaping that future.

Good luck. And don't forget to change your password.

Attack Tools

Attackers use a wide variety of tools to accomplish their objectives. This appendix lists many classes of tools used, as defined by function.

Although it is useful to make clear-cut distinctions for classification purposes, tools may serve multiple purposes and span categories.

Antivirus Defeats

Antivirus defeats are technologies or techniques designed specifically to circumvent antivirus heuristic detection. Some are passive, such as not performing a flagged behavior like opening a network connection. Some rely on "getting Admin" or elevating privileges and then performing actions that are ignored in a privileged context. Still others actively attack the antivirus program itself.

Antivirus defeats are required during the initial access, persistence, and expansion phases of an operation. They are essential to maintaining operational and program security.

Audio/Webcam Recording

Audio and video recording capabilities may be leveraged during the collection and exfiltration phase of an operation. Though it makes headlines, most widespread malware does not bother collecting this type of data. It's usually too much data to exfiltrate and too much to analyze for too little value.

Backdoor

A *backdoor* or *implant* is a piece of software, hardware, or modification to an existing piece of software or hardware that enables the Attacker to circumvent security. Gaining initial access can be a difficult process that may require using ephemeral or temperamental vulnerabilities or relying on a gullible target. A backdoor ensures future access without the hassle.

Backdoors are an essential form of precaution. Their specific features are fundamental to operational security. They come in two main forms: interactive and noninteractive.

Interactive Backdoor

An *interactive backdoor*, enables the Attacker to execute commands, push or pull files, capture screen shots, or perform other actions in near real time. This requires one or more active network connections between the target box and the Attacker's infrastructure. It also requires a human Attacker on the other end of the connection to send instructions.

An interactive backdoor is usually required to expand access, survey, or make any real-time operational decision.

The Poison Ivy RAT (Remote Access Tool) is an example of an interactive backdoor.

Noninteractive Backdoor

A *noninteractive backdoor* is also known as *beaconing malware*. The undesirable program calls out and establishes a connection to a website, mailbox, file drop, chat channel, or other virtual location. It then retrieves and executes any tasking placed there by the Attacker. A beaconing backdoor may also be used for exfiltrating data. Collected data is leaked out over time to one or more locations.

This form of command and control is required to establish a connection with a target behind a firewall, NAT, or other form of network security. It is necessary for persistence within a network.

Noninteractive command and control provides the Attacker with the ability to scale, as a person is not required to drive each implant. It is the most prevalent form of malware.

The Zeus Trojan is an example of a noninteractive backdoor.

Bootkit

A *bootkit* is a specialized backdoor that loads during the computer boot process. Bootkits often can circumvent core operating system security and restrictions because they are loaded before the operating system in the boot process.

Bootkits are a form of deep precaution, as some may even survive the complete reset of a device and fresh reloading of the operating system. Bootkits also help maintain operational security.

Collection Tools

A *collection tool* is a catchall category for any tool that gathers information for exfiltration to the Attacker. A collection tool may collect e-mail, browser history, keystrokes, passwords, images, engineering drawings, word documents, or anything that is stored on or transits a computer. As the name implies, collection tools fulfill the mission objectives for strategic and directed collection.

Exploits

Exploits are pieces of software that leverage a vulnerability in software or hardware to perform a restricted action. Exploits fall into the three basic categories described in the following sections.

Remote Execution

As the name implies, a *remote execution exploit* enables the Attacker to execute code remotely on the target machine. The exploit may be Attacker initiated whereby the Attacker connects into the target machine. These are known as "pure" remote exploits. Exploits may also be target initiated in which the target is required to connect to an Attacker-controlled service. These are known as "client-side" exploits.

Client-side exploits are also known as *malicious server exploits* because they require the Attacker to set up or compromise a server that the target will access. A specialized subclass of malicious server exploits is cross-site scripting vulnerabilities. In these, the Attacker implants code on a third-party site for distribution to potential targets without compromising the security of the site itself.

Remote execution exploits are required for gaining initial access and sometimes for expanding access within a network.

Local Privilege Escalation

A *local privilege escalation* grants the Attacker elevated access to a resource. A common example is escalating from a standard user on Windows to the Administrator or from the Local Administrator to the Domain Administrator.

Local privilege escalations are required to gain the kind of access the Attacker needs to circumvent antivirus or other defensive products, expand access through a network, or install persistently on a computer or device.

Information Disclosure

In an *information disclosure exploit*, the Attacker gains no control over the target computer but rather retrieves what is supposed to be restricted information.

A common information disclosure abuses a poorly configured or insecurely coded website that accesses a back-end database. Through use of weak or poorly secured credentials or a technique called SQL injection, the Attacker can bypass any front-end security and access the database. For example, Andrew Auernheimer, aka "weev," exploited a rather trivial information disclosure vulnerability in an AT&T website that allowed him to retrieve 100,000 iPad users' e-mail addresses.

Information disclosures are used during targeting and initial access. Depending on the operational objective, they may also be the ultimate goal of the operation.

Fuzzer

A *fuzzer* is an automated or semiautomated program for finding vulnerabilities. Fuzzers input randomized data into targeted software or hardware and then check for indications of flaws such as memory leaks and program crashes. A fuzzer's success depends on the quality of the technology tested and how well the fuzzer stresses it.

Fuzzers are a means to economize resources and to increase knowledge. In the worst case, they might reduce the tediousness and resource drain of testing to find simple vulnerabilities. In the best case, they could uncover vulnerabilities that would otherwise not be found.

Hardware-based Trojan

A *hardware-based Trojan* is when a backdoor is implanted directly into the circuitry of the target equipment. This type of tool is what you might think of in an old spy movie where a phone is "bugged." The listeners slipped in during the middle of the night to make some modification to the physical phone to record audio. That sounds almost quaint by today's standards.

The real threat is the Chinese implanting computer chips with backdoors during the manufacturing process,[1] the NSA fashioning malicious USB cables,[2] or some independent researcher making a USB charger that steals wireless keystrokes.[3]

Such tools are masters of operational security. Hardware is simply outside the scope of most defensive security technology. The only saving defensive grace is that hardware Trojans require the Attacker to gain physical access to the target or their supply chain.

Implant

See "Backdoor" earlier in this chapter.

Keystroke Logger

A *keystroke logger*, or *keylogger* for short, captures and records keystrokes as the user types them. Keystroke loggers are one of the most basic offensive tools. They may be general, capturing all key presses, or application specific, capturing only those within a specific program such as a web browser.

Keyloggers are most useful in capturing logins, passwords, and any other information that is entered but not stored on the computer. This information is not only essential for expanding access, but also for maintaining precaution. Keeping an up-to-date list of passwords helps guarantee access.

This tool may also be used for collection, such as grabbing encrypted messages before they are encrypted, or e-mails that are written but never sent or saved.

Network Capture

A *network capture* tool records network traffic to and from a target machine. This is useful during expansion as the Attacker may pull passwords or password hashes out of the connection stream. Network capture tools may also be useful for passively mapping the network by finding e-mail servers, web proxies, and more.

Network Survey

A *network survey* tool maps out both static and dynamic views of a target network. The static map can show computers, their operating systems, configurations, and offered services, as well as networking gear such as routers, firewalls, and Wi-Fi access points. A static map also shows how these various devices are interconnected, the hierarchical organization, the network addresses, subnets, and more. The dynamic part of a network survey includes gathering information on how data is routed into, out of, and through the network; the bandwidth; any mobile or intermittent network clients; the server load; and so on.

Often a network survey requires a variety of tools tailored to profiling specific types of network setups and devices. Maintaining an accurate survey of the network is an ongoing task and fundamental to achieving any level of target awareness.

Network Tunnel

A *network tunneling* tool is required to route data between the Attacker and different segments of a target network. For example, as shown in Figure A.1, many corporate networks have several tiers: a DMZ for Internet-facing servers, a user network, an internal server network, and so on.

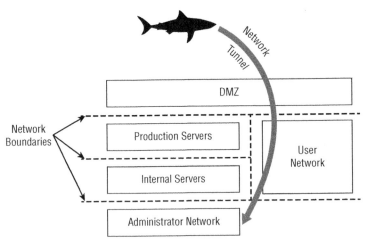

Figure A.1: Network tunneling

Attacker points of access can be anywhere but usually begin either in the DMZ or on the user network. A network tunnel enables Attackers to route through their points of access to an internal end point to expand access or collect data.

Password Dumpers and Crackers

A *password dumper* is a utility that pulls clear text or hashed passwords from a target system. Password dumpers exist for practically every platform, including desktop computers, mobile phones, and a variety of networking equipment.

Hashed passwords are passwords that are run through a one-way mathematical algorithm before being stored. In general, a hashed password is not particularly useful, though there are exceptions. To be useful, the Attacker must recover the original password from the hash.

If the hash is implemented correctly, reversing the hash and recovering the original password is mathematically impossible. Instead, Attackers employ *password crackers*. A password cracker uses a combination of storage, processing power, and intelligent search algorithms to attempt to brute force or guess the original password. For each potential guess, the cracker computes a hash and compares it to the dumped hash. If they match, the Attacker knows the guessed password matches the original.

Password dumpers and crackers are essential to expanding access. A common Attacker tactic is to gain access to an administrator's machine, dump his passwords, and then use the administrator's credentials to move throughout the network.

Packer

A *packer* takes a piece of software; bundles it into a payload; and compresses, encrypts, or otherwise obfuscates that payload. When run, a packed program reverses the process and decompresses, decrypts, and then loads and runs the payload.

Application installers are a simple nonmalicious form of a packer. When the user double-clicks a typical application installer, it decompresses and copies embedded files to the appropriate folders, and then makes any required system or settings changes.

Malicous packers are conceptually no different in function than an application installer, except their purpose is to avoid analysis. Simple packers decrypt everything at once. Advanced packers decrypt portions as needed, leaving only a small portion of the payload visible at any given moment.

Packers provide a way to improve operational security by avoiding antivirus signatures or network filters. They also may improve program security by increasing the cost of analysis, slowing down analysis, and limiting the amount of useful information that can be disseminated.

They do have their downsides, though. The portion of the packer responsible for packing or unpacking the payload may be signatured, leading to a decrease in operational security and a linking of different tools. To counter this defect, Attackers have increasingly resorted to one-off packing utilities or polymorphic code generators.

Persistence Mechanism

A *persistence mechanism* is the method a backdoor, collection tool, or other program uses to start running. It is not a tool, per se, but rather the functionality required to make other tools work. A backdoor is useless if it is never run.

Persistence mechanisms are not inherently malicious. Many are legitimate and thoroughly documented for use by developers. A persistence mechanism may be used by legitimate programs to, for example, provide hardware support, run antivirus scans, check for software updates, perform backups, or more.

Persistence mechanisms operate at several different privilege levels and are run during different parts of the startup process, as shown in Figure A.2. At the lowest level are hardware-based implants. These hook directly into the physical device's startup process.

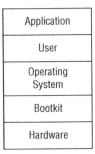

Figure A.2: Persistence levels

The next level up is a *bootkit*, which hooks into the software routines used to load an operating system. The TDL or Alureon rootkit is an example that hijacks a Windows computer's Master Boot Record to load malicious code before the operating system.

Further up the stack are programs that launch when the operating system is booted. There are a wide variety of these on every operating system. On desktop systems, these include drivers, system services, and scheduled tasks. The Windows Firewall is a program launched by an operating system–level persistence mechanism. According to Mandiant, the so-called BISCUIT malware used by APT1 is also a service.

Next, there are user-level persistence mechanisms. These launch when a user logs into the system. The Startup folder on Windows is an example, as is the Login Items setting on Mac. Many versions of malware use user-level persistence mechanisms as a fallback when they do not have sufficient privilege to install at a lower level.

At the highest level are application-specific persistence mechanisms. These are launched with or as part of the specific application. A common legitimate example is a browser plugin, such as Java, that launches when the user visits a certain page. A quasi malicious example are the browser toolbars that many shareware programs install.

The different levels of persistence mechanisms have trade-offs between ease of implementation, potential functionality, and stealth. At the bootkit level, a program could reprogram the operating system to capture user logins, but it will be hard pressed to capture a screen shot. Graphics are running on a completely different level of the technical stack. A hook into user level can easily grab the screen shot, but it will have limited options for stealth. User-level programs do not have many of the privileges required to avoid detection.

Persistence mechanisms are one of the few natural choke points in the Attacker's toolkit. The Attacker needs something to persist to maintain access, even if it only operates intermittently. For this reason, security programs attempt to monitor, detect, and prevent the installation of anything persistent.

A wide variety of persistence mechanisms are essential for maintaining precaution, operational security, and program security.

Polymorphic Code Generator

A *polymorphic code generator* takes computer software in source code or machine code format and transforms it so that the code is changed but the underlying functionality remains the same.

For a trivial example, suppose a program adds three numbers together. Sample code might look like the following:

```
sum = a + b + c
```

This is one way of doing it, but an equivalent action might be

```
sum = b + c + a
```

or even

```
intermediate = (a - 42 + c) * 2
does_not_matter = intermediate * 5
save(does_not_matter)
sum = intermediate/2 + b + 42
...
delete(does_not_matter)
```

The latter set of instructions is inefficient, but it serves the purpose of altering what the generated binary code will be. Different binary code means a different look to static antivirus scanning.

A polymorphic code generator automates a morphing process like this example for entire programs, generating different output programs with the same malicious functionality as the input program.

As detailed by Brian Krebs, some enterprising criminals have even created a moneymaking service out of combining polymorphic code generators, packers, and offline antivirus scanning.

[A] crypting service takes a bad guy's piece of malware and scans it against all of the available antivirus tools on the market today—to see how many of them detect the code as malicious. The service then runs some custom encryption routines to obfuscate the malware so that it hardly resembles the piece of code that was detected as bad by most of the tools out there. And it repeats this scanning and crypting process in an iterative fashion until the malware is found to be completely undetectable by all of the antivirus tools on the market.[4]

—**Brian Krebs**

It's one-stop shopping for all your criminal antivirus circumvention needs.

Code morphing enables the Attacker to maintain some level of program security at reduced cost. With this capability, the capture of one offensive tool may not lead to the compromise of another, even if the two have identical functionality.

Rootkit

A *rootkit* is a program that hides files, network connections, processes, and more. Rootkits provide the stealth necessary to avoid detection and maintain operational security. Though a rootkit may be paired with any offensive tool, it is almost always paired with a backdoor.

Screen Scraper

A *screen scraper*, or *screenshot tool*, is used to capture the image that appears on a user's screen. Screenshots are useful for being aware of what a user or program is doing at a given moment. This functionality has been part of virtually every backdoor for the past 15 years. Screen scrapers are trivial to implement because Windows and Mac have built-in functions for capturing screen output.

System Survey

A *system survey utility* gathers information about one or more computer systems where the Attacker has access. Survey utilities gather a wide variety of information including files, processes, Registry entries (Windows), network shares, installed programs, detailed operating system information, user lists, uptime (the length of time since a system was rebooted), and more.

Survey functionality is often built directly into backdoors or integrated via modules; though it may be a separate utility as well. Survey functionality is critical to target awareness.

Vulnerability Scanner

A *vulnerability scanner* is exactly that, a tool that scans a network for known vulnerabilities. Scanners are dual-use tools, as the Attacker can use them to find vulnerabilities in a potential target while the Defender can use them to locate issues within their own network.

Vulnerability scanners may be combined with an automated exploitation system that instantly exploits any issues found. Immunity Security's Canvas software and Rapid7's Metasploit provide this kind of integrated functionality.

Vulnerability scanners are useful during the targeting and expansion phases of an operation. They may also double as a form of network survey tool, providing target awareness.

References

Chapter 1

1. WikiLeaks statement on the mass recording of Afghan telephone calls by the NSA
   `https://wikileaks.org/WikiLeaks-statement-on-the-mass.html`.

2. Connecting to Opportunity: A Survey of Women's Access to Mobile Technology
   `http://www.usaid.gov/sites/default/files/documents/1871/survey_afghan_women_mobile.pdf`.

3. Leonhard, Robert R. *The Principles of War for the Information Age*. ebook. New York: Ballantine Books. 2000.

4. Duggan, Raymond C. Parks and David P. "Principles of Cyber-warfare". *Proceedings of the 2001 IEEE Workshop on Information Assurance and Security*. WestPoint: United States Military Academy, 2001. 122–125.

5. Clausewitz, Carl von. *On War*. ebook. Trans. Colonel J.J. Graham. The Project Gutenberg, 25 February 2006.

Chapter 2

1. Romanian Hacker Gets 21-Month Sentence for Breaching Subway's Point-of-Sale System
   http://www.wired.com/2013/01/subway-hacking-scam/.

2. Would You Click the Link in This Email That Apparently Tricked the AP?
   http://www.slate.com/blogs/future_tense/2013/04/23/ap_twitter_hack_would_you_click_the_link_in_this_phishing_email.html.

3. How Russian Hackers Stole the Nasdaq
   http://www.businessweek.com/articles/2014-07-17/how-russian-hackers-stole-the-nasdaq.

4. National Institute of Standards and Technology: National Vulnerability Database
   http://web.nvd.nist.gov/view/vuln/statistics.

5. Human errors fuel hacking as test shows nothing prevents idiocy
   http://www.bloomberg.com/news/articles/2011-06-27/human-errors-fuel-hacking-as-test-shows-nothing-prevents-idiocy.

6. Operation SNM: Axiom Threat Actor Group Report
   https://www.novetta.com/wp-content/uploads/2014/11/Executive_Summary-Final_1.pdf.

Chapter 3

1. Bradley Manning in his own words: "This belongs in the public domain."
   http://www.theguardian.com/world/2010/dec/01/us-leaks-bradley-manning-logs.

2. Thumb Drive Security 1L NSA 0
   http://www.networkcomputing.com/storage/thumb-drive-security-snowden-1-nsa-0/d/d-id/1110380?.

3. Clausewitz, Carl von. *On War*. ebook. Trans. Colonel J.J. Graham. Project Gutenberg, 25 February 2006.

4. Your Guide to Good Enough Compliance
   http://www.cio.com/article/2439324/risk-management/your-guide-to-good-enough-compliance.html.

Chapter 4

1. 2013 Data Breach Investigations Report
   `http://www.verizonenterprise.com/resources/reports/rp_data-breach-investigations-report-2013_en_xg.pdf.`

2. The Three Cyber-War Fallacies
   `https://www.usenix.org/conference/usenix-security-11/three-cyber-war-fallacies.`

3. After Arrest of Accused Hacker, Russia Accuses U.S. of Kidnapping
   `http://bits.blogs.nytimes.com/2014/07/08/after-arrest-of-accused-hacker-russia-accuses-u-s-of-kidnapping/?_r=0.`

4. Before We Knew It An Empirical Study of Zero-Day Attacks In The Real World
   `http://users.ece.cmu.edu/~tdumitra/public_documents/bilge12_zero_day.pdf.`

5. Shopping For Zero-Days: A Price List For Hackers' Secret Software Exploits
   `http://www.forbes.com/sites/andygreenberg/2012/03/23/shopping-for-zero-days-an-price-list-for-hackers-secret-software-exploits/.`

Chapter 5

1. Hacker's simple mistake leads to five other arrests
   `http://articles.latimes.com/2012/mar/06/business/la-fi-hacking-arrests-20120306.`

2. FBI Directory: Sony's Sloppy North Korean Hackers Revealed Their IP Address
   `http://www.wired.com/2015/01/fbi-director-says-north-korean-hackers-sometimes-failed-use-proxies-sony-hack/.`

3. Coders Behind the Flame Malware Left Incriminating Clues on Control Servers
   `http://www.wired.com/2012/09/flame-coders-left-fingerprints/.`

4. Update = Restart Issues After Installing MS10-015 and the Alureon Rootkit
   `http://blogs.technet.com/b/msrc/archive/2010/02/17/update-restart-issues-after-installing-ms10-015-and-the-alureon-rootkit.aspx.`

5. NSA secretly hijacked existing malware to spy on N. Korea, others
    `http://arstechnica.com/information-technology/2015/01/nsa-secretly-hijacked-existing-malware-to-spy-on-n-korea-others/`.

6. Equation Group: Questions and Answers
    `https://securelist.com/files/2015/02/Equation_group_questions_and_answers.pdf`.

7. TDSS (TDL4) rootkit has infected millions of PCs
    `https://www.julianevansblog.com/2011/06/tdss-tdl4-rootkit-has-infected-millions-of-pcs.html`.

8. An Analysis of Conficker's Logic and Rendezvous Points
    `http://mtc.sri.com/Conficker/`.

9. Exclusive: secret Assad emails lift lid on life of leader's inner circle
    `http://www.guardian.co.uk/world/2012/mar/14/assad-emails-lift-lid-inner-circle`.

10. DoD News Briefing: Donald Rumsfeld and General Myers
    `http://www.defense.gov/transcripts/transcript.aspx?transcript id=2636`.

Chapter 6

1. Goldman says Google blocked email with leaked client data
    `http://www.reuters.com/article/2014/07/03/google-goldman-leak-idUSL2N0PD2R620140703`.

2. Missed Alarms and 40 Million Stolen Credit Card Numbers: How Target Blew It
    `http://www.bloomberg.com/bw/articles/2014-03-13/target-missed-alarms-in-epic-hack-of-credit-card-data`.

3. Massive Internet mishap sparks Great Firewall scrutiny in China
    `http://www.reuters.com/article/2014/01/22/us-china-internet-idUSBREA0K04T20140122`.

4. Popular Wiretapping Tool Used By Law Enforcement Includes Backdoor with Hardcoded Password
    `https://www.techdirt.com/articles/20140529/06423527389/popular-wiretapping-tool-used-law-enforcement-includes-backdoor-with-hardcoded-password.shtml`.

5. All Adobe Updates
    `http://xkcd.com/1197/`.

6. Google won't fix bug hitting 60 percent of Android phones
   http://arstechnica.com/security/2015/01/google-wont-fix-bug-
   hitting-60-percent-of-android-phones/.

7. Exploit released for vulnerability targeted by Linksys router worm
   http://www.pcworld.com/article/2098520/exploit-released-for-
   vulnerability-targeted-by-linksys-router-worm.html.

8. Hacking Canon Pixma Printers – Doomed Encryption
   http://www.contextis.co.uk/resources/blog/hacking-canon-pixma-
   printers-doomed-encryption/.

9. Schneier, Bruce. *Secrets and Lies: Digital Security in a Networked World.*
   Wiley, 2004.

10. Microsoft does it again, botches KB 2992611 SChannel patch
    http://www.infoworld.com/article/2848574/operating-systems
    /microsoft-botches-kb-2992611-schannel-patch-tls-alert-code-
    40-slow-sql-server-block-iis-sites.html.

11. Insurance giant Anthem hit by massive data breach
    http://money.cnn.com/2015/02/04/technology/anthem-insurance-
    hack-data-security/.

12. Disability Claims Mount Despite Billions Spent
    http://backhome.news21.com/article/paperless/.

13. Malware Analysts Have the Tools to Defend Against Cyber-Attacks, But
    Challenges Remain
    http://www.threattracksecurity.com/resources/white-papers
    /cyber-attacks-internal-challenges-malware-analysts-face.aspx.

Chapter 7

1. State Department's unclassified email systems hacked
   http://www.reuters.com/article/2014/11/17/us-cybersecurity-
   statedept-idUSKCN0J11BR20141117.

2. Equation Group: The Crown Creator of Cyber-Espionage
   http://www.kaspersky.com/about/news/virus/2015/equation-group-
   the-crown-creator-of-cyber-espionage.

3. McRaven, William. *Spec Ops: Case Studies in Special Operations Warfare:
   Theory and Practice.* New York: Presidio Press, 1996.

4. Latest 100 Malware Files
   http://www.exterminate-it.com/malware-files-top100.

5. Chinese Hackers Pursue Key Data on U.S. Workers

http://www.nytimes.com/2014/07/10/world/asia/chinese-hackers-pursue-key-data-on-us-workers.html?_r=0.

6. Bitcoin Thefts Surge, DDos Hackers Take Millions
http://www.darkreading.com/attacks-and-breaches
/bitcoin-thefts-surge-ddos-hackers-take-millions/d/d-id/1112831.

7. U.S. State Department – Hackers still in the Email System
http://securityaffairs.co/wordpress/33982/cyber-crime/us-state-department-hack.html.

8. Politics intrude as cybersecurity firms hunt foreign spies
http://www.reuters.com/article/2015/03/12
/us-cybersecurity-fragmentation-insight-idUSKBN0M809N20150312.

9. Beijing to bar Symantec, Kaspersky anti-virus in procurement: report
http://www.reuters.com/article/2014/08/03/us-china-software-ban-idUSKBN0G30QH20140803.

Chapter 8

1. Symantec Statement Regarding New York Times Cyber Attack
http://www.symantec.com/connect/blogs/symantec-statement-regarding-new-york-times-cyber-attack.

2. Why antivirus companies like mine failed to catch Flame and Stuxnet
http://arstechnica.com/security/2012/06/why-antivirus-companies-like-mine-failed-to-catch-flame-and-stuxnet/.

3. 10,000 Top Passwords
https://xato.net/passwords/more-top-worst-passwords
/#.VDshdNR4pRa.

4. PIN Analysis
http://www.datagenetics.com/blog/september32012/index.html.

5. Anonymous speaks: the inside story of the HBGary hack
http://arstechnica.com/tech-policy/2011/02/anonymous-speaks-the-inside-story-of-the-hbgary-hack/.

6. RSA: SecurID Attack Was Phishing Via an Excel Spreadsheet
https://threatpost.com/rsa-securid-attack-was-phishing-excel-spreadsheet-040111/75099.

7. Twenty Critical Security Controls for Effective Cyber Defense
http://www.sans.org/critical-security-controls/.

8. NSA Community Gold Standard Technical Guidance: Manageable Network Plan

`https://www.nsa.gov/ia/_files/vtechrep/ManageableNetworkPlan`
`.pdf.`

9. History of Classification and Declassification
   `http://fas.org/irp/doddir/doe/history.htm.`

10. Strategies to Mitigate Targeted Cyber Intrusions
    `http://www.dsd.gov.au/infosec/top35mitigationstrategies.htm.`

11. Bit9 and Our Customers' Security
    `https://blog.bit9.com/2013/02/08/bit9-and-our-customers-security/.`

12. Tzu, Sun. *The Art of War*: The Oldest Military Treatise in the World. S.I.:
    Ezreads Publications, LLC, 2009.

Chapter 9

1. To Kill a Centrifuge: A Technical Analysis of What Stuxnet's Creators
   Tried to Achieve
   `http://www.langner.com/en/wp-content/uploads/2013/11/To-kill-`
   `a-centrifuge.pdf.`

2. Reed, Thomas C. *At the Abyss: An Insider's History of the Cold War.*
   New York: Presidio Press, 2005.

3. W32.Stuxnet Dossier
   `https://www.symantec.com/content/en/us/enterprise/media`
   `/security_response/whitepapers/w32_stuxnet_dossier.pdf.`

4. Stuxnet: Victims Zero
   `http://blog.kaspersky.com/stuxnet-victims-zero/.`

5. The Three Cyber-War Fallacies
   `https://www.usenix.org/conference/usenix-security-11`
   `/three-cyber-war-fallacies.`

6. Obama Sped Up Wave of Cyberattacks Against Iran
   `http://www.nytimes.com/2012/06/01/world/middleeast/obama-`
   `ordered-wave-of-cyberattacks-against-iran.html?.`

7. Zetter, Kim. *Countdown to Zero Day: Stuxnet and the Launch of the World's
   First Digital Weapon.* Crown, 2014.

8. 1945: Atomic bomb dropped on Hiroshima
   `http://www.history.com/this-day-in-history/atomic-bomb-dropped-`
   `on-hiroshima.`

9. Stuxnet's Oldest Component Solves the Flamer Puzzle
   `http://labs.bitdefender.com/2012/06/stuxnets-oldest-component-`
   `solves-the-flamer-puzzle/.`

10. Flame: Replication via Windows Update MITM proxy server
    https://www.securelist.com/en/blog/208193566
    /Flame_Replication_via_Windows_Update_MITM_proxy_server.

11. Crypto breakthrough shows Flame was designed by world-class scientists
    http://arstechnica.com/security/2012/06/flame-crypto-
    breakthrough/.

12. Sophisticated Flame Virus Takes Malware to a New Level, Now What?
    http://www.digitaltrends.com/computing/flame-takes-malware-to-
    a-whole-new-level/.

13. Meet 'Flame,' the Massive Spy Malware Infiltrating Iranian Computers
    http://www.wired.com/2012/05/flame/all/.

14. Gauss: Abnormal Distribution
    http://securelist.com/analysis/36620/gauss-abnormal-distribution/.

15. Dragonfly: Cyberespionage Attacks Against Energy Suppliers
    http://www.symantec.com/content/en/us/enterprise/media
    /security_response/whitepapers/Dragonfly_Threat_Against_Western_
    Energy_Suppliers.pdf.

16. The "Red October" Campaign – An Advanced Cyber Espionage Network
    Targeting Diplomatic and Government Agencies
    http://www.securelist.com/en/blog/785/The_Red_October_Campaign_
    An_Advanced_Cyber_Espionage_Network_Targeting_Diplomatic_and_
    Government_Agencies.

17. APT1: Exposing One of China's Cyber Espionage Units
    http://intelreport.mandiant.com/Mandiant_APT1_Report.pdf.

18. APT1 Three Months Later – Significantly Impacted, Though Active and
    Rebuilding
    https://www.mandiant.com/blog/apt1-months-significantly-
    impacted-active-rebuilding/.

19. Operation SNM: Axiom Threat Actor Group Report
    https://www.novetta.com/wp-content/uploads/2014/11/Executive_
    Summary-Final_1.pdf.

Appendix

1. Proof That Military Chips From China Are Infected?
   http://defensetech.org/2012/05/30/smoking-gun-proof-that-
   military-chips-from-china-are-infected/.

2. Your USB cable, the spy: Inside NSA's catalog of surveillance magic
   http://arstechnica.com/information-technology/2013/12/inside-the-nsas-leaked-catalog-of-surveillance-magic/.

3. Keysweeper
   https://github.com/samyk/keysweeper.

4. Antivirus is Dead: Long Live Antivirus
   http://krebsonsecurity.com/2014/05/antivirus-is-dead-long-live-antivirus/.

Bibliography

The first two citations, the works by William McRaven and Robert Leonhard, greatly influenced my approach to this book.

McRaven, William. *Spec ops: Case Studies in Special Operations Warfare: Theory and Practice*. New York: Presidio Press, 1996.

Leonhard, Robert R. *The Principles of War for the Information Age*. ebook. New York: Ballantine Books.

A new approach to China. `http://googleblog.blogspot.com/2010/01 /new-approach-to-china.html`.

Accusations of Chinese Hacking in Coke's Failed Big Deal. `http://dealbook .nytimes.com/2013/02/19/accusations-of-hacking-in-cokes-failed- big-deal/`.

Alger, John I. *The Quest for Victory: The History of the Principles of War*. Westport: Greenwood Press, 1982.

Boyd, John. "Destruction and Creation." 3 September 1976. `http://www .goalsys.com/books/documents/DESTRUCTION_AND_CREATION.pdf`.

Chainmail: A Great Model for a Solid Security Strategy. `http://www.security week.com/chainmail-great-model-solid-security-strategy`.

Chinese Hackers Stole Plans for America's New Joint Strike Fighter Plane, Says Investigations Subcommittee Chair. http://cnsnews.com/news /article/chinese-hackers-stole-plans-americas-new-joint-strike-fighter-plane-says-investigations.

Clausewitz, Carl von. *On War*. ebook. Trans. Colonel J. J. Graham. The Project Gutenberg, 25 February 2006.

Cyber War Will Not Take Place. http://www.tandfonline.com/doi/abs/10 .1080/01402390.2011.608939.

Cyberwar is Coming! http://www.rand.org/pubs/reprints/RP223.html.

A Discourse on Winning and Losing. http://www.ausairpower.net/JRB /intro.pdf.

Department of Defense Strategy for Operating in Cyberspace. http://www .defense.gov/news/d20110714cyber.pdf.

Doctrine for Cybersecurity. http://www.cs.cornell.edu/fbs/publications /publicCYbersecDaed.pdf.

EMERGING CHALLENGE: SECURITY AND SAFETY IN CYBERSPACE. http://www.rand.org/content/dam/rand/pubs/monograph_reports /MR880/MR880.ch10.pdf.

Exploring the Black Hole exploit kit. http://nakedsecurity.sophos.com /exploring-the-blackhole-exploit-kit-14/.

Fighting Fraudulent Transactions. http://www.schneier.com/blog /archives/2006/11/fighting_fraudu.html.

Flamer: Highly Sophisticated and Discreet Threat Targets the Middle East. http://www.symantec.com/connect/blogs/flamer-highly-sophisticated-and-discreet-threat-targets-middle-east>.

Hart, B. H. Liddel. *Strategy*. New York: First Meridian Printing, 1981.

Joint Publication 3-13: Information Operations. http://www.defenseinnovation marketplace.mil/resources/12102012_io1.pdf.

Kaspersky Lab-Municiple Products Local Privilege Escalation Vulnerability. http://www.exploit-db.com/exploits/10484/.

Kournikova computer virus hits hard. http://news.bbc.co.uk/2/hi/science /nature/1167453.stm>.

Leonhard, Robert R. *Fighting by Minutes: Time and the Art of War*. Westport: Praeger Publishers, 1994.

Mitnick, Kevin. *The Art of Deception: Controlling the Human Element of Security*. Indianapolis: Wiley, 2007.

National Cyber Security Framework Manual. `https://ccdcoe.org/multimedia /national-cyber-security-framework-manual.html`.

North Korea denies sinking warship; South Korea vows strong response. `http://www.cnn.com/2010/US/05/19/south.korea.ship/index.html`.

Protecting Your Critical Assets: Lessons Learned from "Operation Aurora." `http://www.wired.com/images_blogs/threatlevel/2010/03/opera-tionaurora_wp_0310_fnl.pdf`.

Sarah Palin's E-Mail Hacked. `http://www.time.com/time/politics/article /0,8599,1842097,00.html`.

Security Awareness Training: It's The Psychology, Stupid! `http://www.security week.com/security-awareness-training-its-psychology-stupid`.

Stuxnet Under the Microscope. `http://www.eset.com/us/resources/white-papers/Stuxnet_Under_the_Microscope.pdf`.

Twelve Principles of DoD Cyber Conflict. `http://ctovision.com/2010/02 /twelve-principles-of-dod-cyber-conflict/`.

U.S. said to be target of massive cyber-espionage campaign. `http://www .washingtonpost.com/world/national-security/us-said-to-be-target-of-massive-cyber-espionage-campaign/2013/02/10/7b4687 d8-6fc1-11e2-aa58-243de81040ba_story.html`.

Why you shouldn't train employees for security awareness. `http://www .csoonline.com/article/711412/why-you-shouldn-t-train-employees-for-security-awareness`.

Index

Printed and bound by CPI Group (UK) Ltd, Croydon, CR0 4YY

11/06/2023

03225862-0001